BRAVING CREATIVITY

BRAVING CREATIVITY

Artists Who Turn the Scary, Thrilling, Messy Path of Change into Courageous Transformation

NAOMI VLADECK

NEW DEGREE PRESS
COPYRIGHT © 2023 NAOMI VLADECK
All rights reserved.

BRAVING CREATIVITY
Artists Who Turn the Scary, Thrilling, Messy Path of Change into Courageous Transformation

ISBN
979-8-88926-709-6   *Paperback*
979-8-88926-710-2   *Digital Ebook*

To brave creatives everywhere.

For Sophie and Levi, the bravest hearts I know.

LEARN MORE ABOUT BRAVING CREATIVITY

Braving Creativity, Artists Who Turn the Scary, Thrilling, Messy Path of Change into Courageous Transformation is an invitation to join other women willing to brave creativity after a big life change.

Make your next transition the bravest one yet. Access the interactive Braving Creativity portal to:

- Download a *Braving Creativity* workbook and other learning resources
- Watch video content to help you create a rich transition process that opens you up to big possibilities
- Watch interviews with women who brave creativity and learn how they cultivate awareness, trust, and ease in the face of uncertainty

Access everything from *Braving Creativity, Artists Who Turn the Scary, Thrilling, Messy Path of Change into Courageous Transformation* here: www.bravingcreativity.com.

Learn more about Braving Creativity and the transformational power of community-supported growth. Request a free coaching session with Naomi here: www.creativitymatterscoaching.com.

CONTENTS

―

PREFACE	11
INTRODUCTION	17

CRISIS — **31**

ANTOINETTE WYSOCKI, *PAINTER*	35
CYNTHIA OLIVER, *SCHOLAR, CHOREOGRAPHER*	43
ELJON WARDALLY, *PLAYWRIGHT*	51
MADDIE CORMAN, *ACTOR, WRITER*	59
SARA JULI, *PERFORMANCE ARTIST*	69

GRIEF — **81**

JULIA MANDLE, *MIXED MEDIA INSTALLATION ARTIST*	85
CHIE FUEKI, *PAINTER*	93
L M FELDMAN, *PLAYWRIGHT*	101

DESIRE	**111**
DIPIKA GUHA, *PLAYWRIGHT*	115
YANIRA CASTRO, *INTERDISCIPLINARY ARTIST*	125
ADA PILAR CRUZ, *SCULPTOR*	135
OPPORTUNITY	**145**
ADELE MYERS, *CHOREOGRAPHER*	149
MARTA RENZI, *FILMMAKER*	159
ABIGAIL AND LILY CHAPIN, *SINGER SONGWRITERS*	167
MEGAN WILLIAMS, *CHOREOGRAPHER*	175
SCARY, THRILLING, MESSY THOUGHTS	**187**
ACKNOWLEDGMENTS	197
APPENDIX	201

PREFACE

---

*. . . bravery is not about being fearless, because I wasn't fearless.
But in walking with the fear—and through it
when everything I thought I knew
turned out to be flimsy and questionable.
And as I walked through it all, there was revelation,
and there was confusion, and there was discovery.*

—KRISTA TIPPETT

On stage for a storytelling series at the Casa del Sol, a Mexican restaurant in Nyack, NY, I shared the story of my first sexual encounter as a widow. My clitoris had awakened from a long slumber, and it was hell-bent on action. I needed to be touched. "Tonight will be nothing of the old!" I declared as I unhooked my bra at the end of the night and barreled into bed with a man I had flirted with in college twenty-five years earlier. I was enthusiastic, but, as I told the audience, "I had no idea what I was in for." As I described the night—the prowl, the flirtation, the surprisingly varied dirty talk—women from my bereavement group hooted from the front row. I continued, "When I arrived home from the date, I headed straight to bed in my coat and shoes and slid under the covers. I let go of everything I was holding. Which, at that moment, was the pure searing pain of absence."

My husband, Eric, was never coming back, and that sex was absolute proof that it was true.

How could I have known my feverish desire for sex was actually grief pushing against the walls of my heart, looking for an exit but finding no way out? In the writing, in the performing, and in the reception of that piece, I began to feel a shift. I heard a part of me whisper, "Wow, *that* was brave."

That single whisper of acknowledgment to myself was the catalyst for what would become this book nearly eight years later. More than one artist I've interviewed for their story has reported hearing a version of "Wow, you are brave" after they created something of their own from the ashes and then shared it with the public.

My sense is that if you are *perceived* as brave, it's because you have stirred someone else's longing for the courage they imagine you have. But if you *feel* brave, it's because you have traveled a broad expanse of the unknown and have arrived on solid ground when at least a part of you feared you might vanish altogether.

I grew curious about my decision to process my grief headlong in that performance and at that time. In that moment, I sensed I had stepped through the looking glass and onto a path that was unfolding with some mysterious purpose.

I often felt lost in the time after Eric's death. But if I wasn't lost, then where was I?

To locate myself, I needed to understand my relationship to change. For answers, I looked to artists I admired. I have spent my life among creatives. As a theater artist, arts administrator, nonprofit founder, and coach, I knew there was something to learn from the uncertainty we associate with the creative process that so precisely reflected this space I was now in—or in-between—in my life.

I wondered how artists grappled with big change. Did they reckon, as I did after Eric's death, with terror, confusion, and uncertainty? With only the faint and distant promise of renewal, how did they light their way through that darkness? *Why did they?*

I looked behind me too. My mother was twenty-two when she had my twin brother and me, with my younger brother following shortly afterward. She was a nurse at the time she married my father, a surgical resident, after six months of dating. She stayed at home with us, but her heart was in making things. When my two brothers and I were kids, she'd stop at roadside discards to cut open the back of a couch and look for "treasure," refinish furniture, make the cover art for our middle-school book reports, and tackle any project for an excuse to run to the hardware or craft store.

She created art too, from large-scale stained-glass windows to meticulously beaded jewelry. She worked in nearly every medium known to humankind with assuredness, but there was a point in her process when she would come to a grinding halt. Perhaps she didn't have the courage to go further or was afraid of the choices she'd have to make if she did. I always knew when retreat was imminent because she'd become agitated and self-critical.

Our home had multiple turbulences, but the one I watched most closely was my mother's. She often said "Don't rock the boat." I undertook to soothe the seas that worried my little-kid heart in ways I sensed might stop the rocking so we would stay steady and nothing would change.

I became a great fixer and pleaser, which has its advantages but also its costs. I struggled to know my own feelings and express my own needs. I thought I was afraid of separation because I feared new places and circumstances. In my thirties, I realized there was something even scarier to me than any of that. Underneath the story of my fear was *a belief* that something would happen to my family without me there to attend to *them*.

Eric's alcoholism and death put an end to the illusion that I could steady anyone else's boat with sheer determination. But in this new reality, who was I? And who would I become?

I heard a whisper in my heart. I recognized its message from other endings in my life. In the past, my heart said I had the courage to embrace uncertainty during pivotal inflection points—choosing to study Japanese theater, start a nonprofit, quit my "real" job to become a coach—and it whispered to me after Eric's death. *I have the courage to walk the scary, thrilling, messy path of this transition.* I did not know what possibilities would rise to meet me along the way. I just had to engage with the *process* and trust that I would arrive somewhere different than the painful place I was starting from.

Change is a catalyst that will eventually rock your boat—a crisis, a need that clamors to be met, a chance to try something new. Endings and beginnings are as natural an occurrence in our lives as they are in nature. That fact, however, does not assuage our fear of change or make the journey any less arduous.

The artists in these stories have a facility with transition. They are practiced at hanging out in that fertile "in-between" space for as long as it takes for something to shift. But also, and more importantly, they understand the creative function of time spent in transition. They activate this empty space by making courageous choices along the way that produce new insights and synchronicities that open them up to new possibilities. *This is the work of Braving Creativity.*

That night, when I performed at Casa del Sol, I was validating the worth of all of who I was then—the grieving, yes, but also the angry and irreverent parts, the fearful and libidinous parts, and the foul-mouthed parts. Looking at our shadows to bring them into the light and share what emerges in word, in paint, in body and in music is the power of all creative artists.

Inside of this book are fifteen stories, in addition to my own. I've studied with or worked with several of these women over the years, and I've followed their lives and artistry since. Others are new connections via family and friends, women willing to share their perspective on making art after a big life change.

The stories that follow begin with a turning toward the unknown when the stakes were as high as the threat of an illness or the end of a marriage. The catalysts vary from crisis to desire for growth and opportunity to time spent in grief. The change that catalyzes the transition process they embark upon isn't always visible in the work they create, although in some stories, there is an obvious convergence. I'll also introduce the five transformational pillars I use in my coaching practice. These pillars are pulled from my own life experience and help to identify ways to ignite our creativity inside of a process of transition to stimulate your courage for growth after a big life change changes everything.

This book grew from my desire to process my husband's struggle, as well as my mother's. It is also my offering to creative women and all creatives who struggle to be brave. I long to champion you to say the things you must say and make the work you are called to make so you can also hear a version of "Wow, you are brave!" and know it to be true.

INTRODUCTION

That which we want to outrun
will not lose its power over us until we can be with it,
creative work will go deeper and contain more vibrancy
if we stop trying to avoid something
we do not want to face about the self or the world.
—ORIAH MOUNTAIN DREAMER

On September 8, 2015, I arrived home with my seven-year-old son and ten-year-old daughter after their first day of school. Our three-year-old hound-lab mix, Puck, dashed between our legs and dug his snout into the pile of bags and backpacks I dropped at the front door. The kids dispersed, and without a pause, I shifted into my evening routine. I called Puck toward the back door to let him out and noticed he had pooped by the door. He'd never done that before. I remember thinking, *This is not a problem, Naomi. You're doing great. Look at everything you did today. And the kids? They seem great, don't they? Everything is* great.

I hadn't heard from my husband for twenty-four hours. The night before, I packed a jumbo pack of tissue boxes, pre-sharpened pencils, glue sticks, and every other item on the second- and fifth-grade school supply list into "his" and "her" bags. I prepared lunches and supervised showers and told the kids they'd speak to Daddy before bed, but they didn't ask about it before I tucked them in and I didn't remind them. I checked my cell phone—nothing.

That next morning, I'd captured a blurry photo of my daughter racing to the bus wearing a rainbow beret. I headed to my son's first-grade assembly, where he sat on the gymnasium floor in a Minecraft T-shirt looking over the shoulder of a classmate who held a stuffed animal folded face down in his lap.

Around noon, I'd texted Eric: When you disappear like this, I think you might be dead.

By midday, I still hadn't heard from him. With his CPAP on, I wondered, was it possible he didn't hear his phone?

Eric and I met a few months into the eleventh grade. We often marveled at our good luck during our twenty-nine years together. Now, over the past two months, erratic communication had become the norm. He had been staying in a vacant two-bedroom house owned by his grandmother that was just a few miles from our home, accessible by a bridge over the Hudson River. By then, it had been emptied of countless tchotchkes and the dozens of teddy bears that once occupied an entire couch in the small sitting room at the front of the house. Gone, too, were bags of costume jewelry, cups, and glassware she picked up at yard sales and for which she had no place and no purpose either.

A few weeks earlier, Eric called me to tell me his father had been there. He was shaken because his father woke him up berating him. He described himself cowering in a corner of the room. His father demanded that he "stop this" and "fix that." This was his father's prescription for everything. *Just do it.*

Eric asked me on that call if I would bring a toiletry bag with his blood pressure medication, which he accidentally left behind. When I entered, I heard the CPAP machine loudly whirling, pushing air in and out of the mask in the upstairs room where he was sleeping. Everything inside that small house, from the smell of the bedroom to the sound of pulsing CPAP machine to the darkness of the paneled walls, felt stifling. It was a beautiful day outside, and I wanted the air and light around me. I woke him gently and asked him to step outside, and we moved to the small deck outside the kitchen.

"You're a sight for sore eyes," he said, standing just feet away from me in underwear and a T-shirt. He was trembling, and his face was raw and bloated. It was around six o'clock. When he spoke, tears came to his eyes. I felt his terror and rose to comfort him, and he gently stroked my back. After a moment, I pulled away. When I asked if he had a ride to a meeting that night, he turned back toward the house. We both knew he wouldn't be going.

The kids were emptying their backpacks of colored flyers and lunch bags when Puck barked at the back door. After

I cleaned up the mess he had left and let him back in, the phone rang. "Naomi, we're with Eric." My husband's younger brother, Phil, was on the phone. "The EMTs are here. Can you get here now?" he asked as I doled out Pepperidge Farm Goldfish Crackers and sliced apples. His request sounded so perfunctory. I protested quietly to myself. *No, I can't just get there.* Inside my rebuttal was anger. I was so angry at Eric for making me choose again, between him and this disease and between my children and going to him.

I spoke with an addiction counselor after Eric returned from rehab a year earlier. I was standing in front of a large rectangular window in our home, looking out toward the river during the late fall as dry leaves swept across the frame. The counselor was teaching me how to construct a boundary sentence. I grabbed a piece of paper and a pen and tried to keep up. "First, the '*if statement*.' Okay, got it. Then what? *Oh yeah, the consequence.*"

"They are working on him," Phil continued. I envisioned Eric's family encircling him in the middle of his grandmother's tiny kitchen. I told Phil I'd try to get someone to stay with kids and hung up. My boundaries became porous. I sent a text to a nearby friend to see if she would be available to come over while I was gone.

The phone rang again. It was my sister-in-law, calling from her home. "Naomi, did Phil call you?" she asked. "It's not good."

To anyone else, it would have been obvious what she was trying to tell me, but my mind was enmeshed in a rant. *I can't get there. I can't get to you. I want to get to you. But I can't. I can't help you.*

My friend texted to say she was on her way, and the phone rang again. My father-in-law was calling from his car on the bridge. He was on his way to my house.

"Naomi," he said clearly before breaking down. "We lost him."

The tear that began moments before now ripped fully open and out of my body came a wail. I didn't have time to contain it. My kids were standing right there.

I hung up the phone. My son and I were both sobbing. He latched onto my side, and I hobbled with him over to the sofa. My daughter had disappeared. I called my friend. "I can't find Sophie." I gasped. "I found her," my friend said. "We're at the bottom of the driveway."

Two days later, I put my mother and my children into my Subaru and drove us across that same bridge to the funeral service. When I pulled the car in front of the church, I realized I couldn't just drop my children off and leave them to go park the car because they were glued to me. My son wrapped his arms around my waist the second we got the phone call that Eric had died and hadn't let go. My daughter had ditched her beret for thick black eyeliner and a fake nose ring and was no way in hell going to budge without me.

It didn't even occur to me—nor did anyone suggest—that perhaps it was not the best idea or even appropriate to drive myself to my own husband's funeral. I made most of the arrangements with my mother-in-law. How did it come to pass that I left out that detail?

Four days before Eric died, on September 4, he'd checked himself into the hospital. He was attempting to detox on his own when his symptoms started to scare him enough to seek help. He reported feeling numbness in his fingers and pain in his chest. They admitted him, and he stayed for twenty-four hours. On September 7, he returned to the emergency room after waking up on the kitchen floor with a bloody face. He was there only a few hours before they discharged him. He died that night, the night before the first day of school.

After he died, I tried to piece together what happened during those few days. When I returned home with the hospital records, I noticed a page missing. The following day, I went back to the records room. I took the missing page into the small dark chapel that was adjacent and sat in a pew. There it was: A.M.A. scribbled on the progress chart note from his first visit. He'd left the hospital against medical advice. *I will do this myself* and *I will do this my way* are what I imagined Eric thinking. Those were the expectations he was trying to fulfill. The part of him that screamed *stop it* and *fix it. Just do it.* It wasn't the first time he'd left the hospital against medical advice during the prior two years, but this final time stabbed me. A younger part of me—the part that tied my worth to my ability to keep others safe—felt enormous grief at my failure. *I alone was not enough.*

My husband's death catalyzed a transition that began in that small chapel in an instant, but my own process of recovery and growth would take years. Shifting from one identity and one set of beliefs and patterns to another is not something that can be commanded or that we can be shamed into undertaking. We are hard wired to protect our most vulnerable parts at all costs and by any means necessary. No one can "just do" the hard work of change.

In *Wired to Create*, Scott Barry Kaufman and Carolyn Gregoire cite research on positive psychological growth after trauma. "People naturally develop and rely on a set of beliefs and assumptions that they've formed about the world, and in order for growth to occur after trauma, the traumatic event must deeply challenge those beliefs" (Kaufman and Gregoire 2016, 93).

Big change invites you on a path to brave creativity, beginning with the deep and vulnerable places in your heart. That is where this book's journey begins.

At some time in your life, you will experience a crisis, a burning desire to grow beyond your current experience, or a life-changing opportunity. While, on paper, growth sounds promising, the reality of the path ahead is not always a warm and fuzzy one. You'll first be asked to turn over all identifying credentials because you are on your way to "destination unknown" where you realize you are not the same person you were before. You will feel naked and vulnerable as you turn further away from your old life and toward a future where nothing has yet been written.

Most people do not allow change to *change them*. We resist in every imaginable way so we can hold on to even a hair's width of our current status quo life rather than turn toward a future we cannot see. Unknown territory feels risky because, while anything is possible, nothing is certain. When I interviewed author of *Coaching the Artist Within*, psychotherapist, educator, and creativity coach Eric Maisel, he said, "Some artists are willing to take risks, but most people are not willing to take risks. Most people don't grow. Most artists don't grow. They repeat themselves."

If you are reading this book, my guess is you are among the risk-curious creatives. Had I understood the wisdom in uncertainty when I was younger, perhaps I'd have spent less time grasping for control and more time embracing the uncharted path l often found myself upon. Life coach and author of *Follow Your North Star*, Martha Beck, says, "If you've ever been through a life change, you know that emerging into a new life is not easy. It's exhausting. It's scary, you feel vulnerable, things can go wrong. It seems to take forever, but that struggle itself creates the kind of health and tenacity and robustness that's going to enable you to sustain a positive change in a really powerful way" (Beck 2005, 8:48).

The real opportunity in change takes place when we get curious about what will emerge in the place of our former identity. Whatever we encounter in this empty space is now part of a process of transition where we will discover who we are now that our old life has ended and move toward who we are longing to become.

The late William Bridges, organizational change theorist and author of *The Way of Transition*, talks about the importance of keeping an open mindset in the face of uncertainty because it is in that space that "people gain access to their deeper creative energies and impulses" (Bridges 2001, 38). Artists who choose growth grapple with their material through play, dialogue, and experimentation. They learn to endure periods of anxiety and self-doubt because they understand they are in a process whose function is simply the freedom to create anything. They trust in the process enough to enter the empty space in transition with nothing and allow something to unfold.

Imagine if you believed the grief, sweetness, wisdom, and courage in your shadows would be met by people, experiences, and insights you could not before have imagined you would find. Wouldn't you brave creativity despite the fear of all that you can't know from where you are standing now?

Before we go any further, I want to share an anecdote with you to tempt you forward into the great unknown. If you pay attention in transition, there will be moments when you sense more than just the empty space around you. If you surrender to all that you don't know right now, your heart will open, as will all of your senses. In that state, you will have experiences that surprise you for their inexplicable synergy and truth.

When I was in my mid-twenties, I was lost. Without the certainty and validation that education provided, I had no familiar compass to gauge my direction. No destination to exert my effort toward, no place to go that felt right or true. One weekend during that time, I sat in the back row of a theater and watched the Suzuki Company of Toga (SCOT) perform *Electra* entirely in Japanese. I don't speak Japanese. As the theater emptied around me, I remained, crying. But I wasn't sad. I felt seen *through*; not past me but seen so deeply that it touched me in this overwhelming way that was both so sad and also so filled with love. *Something* happened to me that night. The energy that moved between the stage and my body ignited a courage I didn't know I had before. *Everything changed after that.*

My heart, body, and mind pointed me in a new direction that had no purpose or plan I could name. I wasn't interested in becoming an actor, but I joined a nine-month residency with American members of the Suzuki company. Training with the company transformed my fear into something else. This shift was only apparent to me, and yet the impact on my life was huge. It gave me the courage to make choices that were outside of my reach before—to move to New York City and to go to graduate school, to name two.

Before that night in the theater, *I had no idea what to do with my life.*

Big change is a wake-up call, and the transition that follows has the potential to open us to receive the energetic subtleties around us. If you stay open and pay attention, one of those experiences might ignite your courage to take a risk. In her book, *The Art of Resonance*, theater director and author Anne Bogart says, "In order to resonate with something, I have to attend fully to it, with an openness to being affected, influenced, and literally moved… To be on the receiving end of resonance… requires a certain disposition, a specific way of relating to the world" (Bogart 2021, 13-14). Your response to big change may just be what creates that "certain disposition" in you to be moved by the courage in the stories within these pages.

The path to transformation is so layered and so complex. And yet I believe it is an imperative deserving of a lifetime of curious effort.

———

FIVE PILLARS OF BRAVING CREATIVITY

In my work with artists, I talk about five pillars of transformation. I'll share the broad themes of each pillar with you here before illuminating how each artist has danced with and in-between these pillars on their brave creative path after big change.

LIBERATE

The practice of liberation is the first creative opportunity after big change. You can't get far into a transformational process by ignoring the beliefs and thoughts that formed the foundation of your old life. The key to addressing limiting beliefs once you become aware of them is to practice self-compassion. Self-compassion is the ability to bring curiosity and care to the beliefs, experiences, or thoughts sabotaging your desire for authentic expression and connection. You will become skillful at noticing limiting beliefs and thoughts when they arise and be able to replace them with ones aligned with the wisdom in your heart.

Key Concept: Self-awareness and Self-compassion

NAVIGATE

To navigate is the skill of listening to your heart and sensing where you want to go. Navigation pulls its wisdom from your intuition, from your body's store of knowledge, and from the synergies in the world around you. You will learn how to shift from feeling overwhelmed and confused to staying grounded in the truth of your heart. The practice of listening to and receiving your inner wisdom has such a clarifying impact because it gives you confirmation that you are going in the right direction when you can't actually know where you are headed.

Key Concept: Listening and Receiving

PLAY

Play is the workhorse of transition, and its engine is curiosity. As you practice these pillars, you'll shift from believing your efforts are wasteful or stupid to embracing a playground of options to try. The *process* of discovery is the most valuable aspect of play, and the most creative. In play, you will test assumptions, experiment with actions, and acquire the proof of your courage to take risks *regardless of the outcomes*. Play cultivates fortitude to endure the uncertainty inherent in any discovery process.

Key Concept: Curiosity and Experimentation

EMPOWER

When you enter the realm of empowerment, you are becoming the author of your life. You can now declare your worth and use language to express your values and purpose. You are willing to take risks to assert your presence and your voice. In empowerment, you move from doing the hard work of change alone to resourcing yourself with the support and care of other people who recognize and affirm your worth. When you feel empowered in this way, you share your knowledge and passion, and you assert your autonomy when you need to stand alone.

Key Concept: Declare, Share, and Resource

FLOURISH

When you journey through transition after a big change, you learn to trust in yourself and in a universe that makes it possible for you to flourish. In flourishing, you build a runway of opportunities that align with the truth in your heart. These opportunities will ignite unplanned and synergistic occurrences that will feel like magic. You will instill what you learn with each experience and celebrate your courage to brave your creative path every day.

Key Concept: Trust, Instill, and Celebrate

If you have grown up at all change-averse or have been at all afraid of rupture and of empty space (and who has not at some point in their lives?), the stories that follow will assure you that there is a process and a function to the seeming incoherency of transition. I believe we can find joy and gratitude in the dynamic creative process that is activated after a big change, which is the path of the brave creative.

CRISIS

The Chinese word for crisis is made up of two pictures, danger and opportunity.

—DR. JEAN SHINODA BOLEN

When everything you know ceases to exist, you will have trouble computing your current reality. The assumptions that formed the basis of your operating system will go haywire. Everything that comes into your visual field will now be processed through this confusion. Every conversation you have at the grocery store, every time you brush your teeth, every girls' night out will now be filtered through an *identity that is in crisis*.

The stories in this section all begin with a crisis event, but what follows is less a discussion of the crisis itself and more about the crisis of identity that comes after. Whether by illness, by accident, by separation, or disaster, a crisis ends something. Endings at that magnitude trigger a breaking down of our old identity that will be met, at times, with denial, terror, acceptance, relief, or even optimism. As despairing, disorienting, and lonely as you will feel after a crisis blows up your life, you will, presumably, still have to function in some capacity. You will have to pay your bills, take care of your children, or go to the grocery store. You will want to go back to the way things were before, only what you seek isn't behind you anymore, and it isn't anywhere in sight either.

You will rage against change, and at some point, you will, if you persist, soften to your new reality. And when you do, you will arrive somewhere else. That new place isn't yet a panacea, Oz, or any kind of heaven you might have dreamed of as a little girl. That new place is exactly where you are, just further along on your path. And being further along means you have made some choices that excite the possibility that something new and meaningful will arise to pull you another few steps toward the still unknowable future. Author, award-winning journalist, and speaker Suleika Jaouad, in her TED Talk *What Almost Dying Taught Me About Living*, says, "Every single one of us will have our life interrupted, whether it's by the rip cord of a diagnosis or some other kind of heartbreak or trauma that brings us to the floor. We need to find ways to live in the in-between place, managing whatever body and mind we currently have" (Jaouad 2019, 16:00).

I wouldn't wish a crisis on anyone, but I can tell you there are gifts to be found in transition. Gratitude is one. It showed up so early after my husband's death that I was almost ashamed to mention it to anyone. I was grateful to Eric for the chance to move beyond the moment we were stuck in because there was no evidence in sight that it would turn out any other way than it did. Let me be clear, I wish it weren't so, but that was our reality. When the crisis made the choice for us, I chose to be grateful for the chance to grow beyond my circumstances and bigger than my fear.

There is another gift too. Some of the artists call it "optimism," some call it "faith," some refer to it as a "trust in the Universe." Whatever you call that gift, it has a profound energetic impact on our ability to endure in uncertain times. It reflects the "radical, dangerous hope" that fuels our courage to someday do the thing that scares us the most right now (Jaouad 2019). When a crisis disrupts our life, it is certainly a wonder we can function at all. But what is also true is that what seemed impossible to us before, now becomes something we have the audacity to hope for when braving creativity toward our own transformation.

In the stories that follow, see if you can identify moments of creativity that ignite these artists' courage to make choices that catalyze new possibilities, insight, and growth. You will hear from five artists who share stories of how they turned from crisis toward a creative process and found new meaning, identity, and purpose in their lives. Antoinette Wysocki shows us how she broke through the painful denial that interfered with her healing after a traumatic injury to her painting hand; Eljon Wardally's sudden stroke at the age of twenty-nine provokes her courage to commit to a bigger vision for her creative life; Actor Maddie Corman commits to writing her first play, which delves into her own experience of a traumatic event in her marriage; Cynthia Oliver reveals how a collaboration made it possible to explore how her cancer diagnosis and recovery changes her story; Sara Juli chooses to create a performance piece that reveals and also releases the childhood beliefs that threatened to destroy her marriage.

ANTOINETTE WYSOCKI

If I don't get something out creatively, it will eat me alive. It's just something I have to do.

—ANTOINETTE WYSOCKI, PAINTER

"No, no, no!" The words formed a silent scream in Antoinette Wysocki's mind as a pickup truck hit her car head-on. *I have so much more to do*, she thought. *This is not how I'm going to go out!* While the accident didn't take her life, Antoinette suffered a critical injury to her right hand, which was on the steering wheel at the time of impact. "It's my painting hand."

For the first four months of recovery, she resisted feeling the full extent of the pain that her injury wrought. The doctors questioned why Antoinette rated her pain low on the assessment scale she was given each week. Succumbing to the pain meant acknowledging the possibility that she'd never paint again and lose everything she built her life upon as an artist. Her extreme resistance was accompanied by punitive thoughts that sabotaged her recovery effort. Thoughts like *Don't be weak, man up!* ultimately resulted in her feeling depressed and alone. "I just wasn't allowing anyone to help me."

Raised by a single working mom, Antoinette describes her childhood as "Not so great." She spent much of her young life either tucked away under her mother's desk, drawing or in her own little world. Her mom believed women have no choice but to take care of themselves to survive, always emphasizing that "You can't depend on anyone."

Antoinette inherited that belief and her fierce work ethic from her mother and stepmother. After graduating with a BFA from the San Francisco Art Institute, Antoinette exhibited in over two dozen solo shows all over the United States and internationally in London, Dubai, Seoul, and Hong Kong, and has works in museum collections. She has also participated in over fifty group exhibitions and has received many private commissions. To support herself, Antoinette worked full-time in education, branding, and fashion. After working during the day, she spent her nights in the studio. "I never wanted to be a starving artist, and I like nice things, so I was practical and I worked hard."

From the contemporary art world, Antoinette received the tacit message that women who choose to be mothers are not true artists. "I've always been defensive about that, particularly after I had children." As a result, she habitually resisted any change that would undermine her commitment to her art.

Becoming a parent forced her to test the assumption that she couldn't be a mother and have a successful career as an artist. When her kids were young, she tried to maintain a late-night studio practice, but eventually, she changed her schedule to work during the daylight hours because, she said, "You can't parent and be exhausted all the time."

The first time Antoinette picked up a paint brush after the accident, she was devastated to find she had lost the fine motor skills in her fingers and wrist. It was her children she turned to once she got permission to go back into her studio after her first surgery. Instead of allowing her fear to keep her from trying to paint, Antoinette used a strategy that has always been central to her art-making—play. "I had my ten-year-old son sit with me in the studio so I could understand that I wasn't trying to make something serious, that I was playing and he was playing with me," she said. This is how Antoinette says she "tricked" herself into beginning. But she also said there was "a big part of me that knew I'd figure it out."

During periods when she was recovering from surgery and couldn't paint, Antoinette spent time looking through her old work at a slow pace, without the pressure of what she referred to as "gallery voices in my head." She described a feeling of liberation that began to let loose in her body, and she had the realization that, before the accident, her practice had gotten to a point where it was meticulous, even calling it "tight." And now, after taking this space to reflect, she had the thought "Maybe this is my opportunity to play."

About five months into her recovery and after playing with paint for about a month, an idea started to emerge. It was something she'd filed away, not thinking she'd ever come back to it. In an old shop "in the middle-of-nowhere Virginia," she says, she found several large early eighteenth-century lithographs of religious iconography. "They kind of cracked me up," she recalled. Because Antoinette was raised Catholic, the images were immediately familiar. She showed the images to one of her sons, who, having no religious education and therefore no context in which to interpret them, questioned certain elements like the eyes that gaze piously toward the heavens. "Why is she rolling her eyes, Mom?" he asked.

It was his reaction and her own curiosity about the iconography that led her to bring the images into the studio to paint a series of portraits using the lithographs as inspiration. She set a specific intention before she started painting them, which was to have fun. "I used to be so worried about the outcome, but with this project, I just wanted to have fun with it." Antoinette was pleased with the result. She decided to push the concept further by adding contemporary iconography with designer branded accessories from Gucci, Crocs, and Adidas. The paintings required Antoinette employ the kind of motor control required of portraiture, which she hadn't tried since before the accident.

Finally, having completed the most technically difficult painting in the series, she was about to sign the piece when she decided to touch up the top of the portrait. Her hand shook. The brush fell, dripping black enamel paint down the face of the image. "You can't get that off," she said. Overcome with emotion, she turned away from the painting with her hands over her face and ran into her backyard. She let out a scream. When she caught her breath, she returned to the studio and, to her surprise, her thirteen-year-old son was standing there. "I wasn't sure what he saw, so I searched for what lesson I could ascribe to what he might have seen. I want him to know my frustration is important to express but also that mistakes aren't everything to me."

For the first time in a while, she allowed the anger around her injury to rise out of her. She had gotten good at entering the studio and not comparing herself to what came before. But when that happened, "there was no way not to face the reality of my injury. If I continue to expect the same result as before the accident, it's just going to be a disaster for me."

Eight months into what would be a series of surgeries and recoveries, Antoinette still gets triggered when someone suggests she learn to paint with her left hand. "It seems ridiculous," she said, when she thinks about switching hands after thirty years of using her right hand successfully. A part of her, however, is willing to allow for the possibility. "If I were to be completely honest with myself," she said with a laugh, "yes, this would be a great time to experiment and just throw down color-field paintings and have fun with something using my left hand."

She's not quite there though. "I haven't become enlightened by the accident. I still think it's a pretty harsh way to learn a lesson. But, if anything has come in terms of a gift, I would say that now I know that I don't function completely independently and that I do have to rely on people. I am not Superwoman. And it's okay to ask for help."

Just when Antoinette thinks she has surrendered as far as she can to the pain and messiness of this transitional time, she is being tested. "I was invited to design a ninety-two-foot public art mural." The mural was something she was looking forward to and even in the early stages of her recovery thought it might be feasible. "I considered every possible way I could accept that commission. But I had to decline it." She had to let go, she said. "It was devastating, but I was able to breathe through that moment. I told myself that this opportunity would come again. I will work again."

Instead of believing that declining the project was "a traumatic failure of mine," she is choosing to get curious. She is asking "Why now? What's the lesson here?" Learning to approach this crisis with curiosity and self-compassion has been the path to accepting whatever shows up each time she approaches the canvas. Now that some time has passed, she's okay with not knowing how things will turn out. That's because she knows in her heart she has so much more to do.

BRAVING CREATIVITY

Liberate and play are the pillars that help us understand how Antoinette is transforming her relationship to fear by testing her courage to embrace her vulnerability and stay open to possibilities that before seemed unfathomable.

LIBERATE

We can all agree that resistance by denial is an ineffective strategy, but that doesn't mean it doesn't make sense when we are in crisis. It's human to turn away from pain, especially when it comes at you as fast as a car crash. The toughness and grit Antoinette believed was a requirement for her success as an artist came from a part of her that rejected her vulnerability with blame and shame-filled thoughts. She defended so vehemently against her new reality because of the underlying belief that needing help was a deal-breaking liability.

After a time though, she softened. She questioned the assumption that asking for help is a sign of weakness. She replaces limiting thoughts like "Don't be weak" and "This is a failure of mine" with new ones like "It's okay to ask for help,"

"I will work again," and "Mistakes aren't everything to me." What is exciting about this transformation is the burgeoning awareness that perhaps there is a larger lesson here that wants to emerge. You can sense a softening that makes it possible to meet her fear with acceptance. Still, in all transitions of this magnitude, there are layers of surrender. Just when we think we have given over enough control to the Universe to do its part, we realize we are still doing more than our share.

PLAY
Antoinette naturally gravitates to play as a strategy for beginning again in small brush strokes to safely test her new reality. She also names and sets an intention: to play. This intention gives her permission to focus on what she can control under these new conditions and not on all that she can't.

She also spends time in reflection and creative contemplation to help her integrate and instill all that she has been processing since the accident about her career as an artist. During a post-surgical pause, a new idea is sparked, which is the result of a question that now has room to grow: Without the pressure of "gallery voices" in my head, what would I create? How will I create? She names and sets a new intention with this project: "to have fun." In this liberating and evolving creative process, she regains her sense of agency and a hopeful vision for her future.

Fear that the disaster would end her career transforms into acceptance of the real challenges she faces and a sense that when the next right opportunities arise, she'll be ready to meet them.

HOW DO YOU BRAVE CREATIVITY?

What beliefs can you liberate yourself from as a result of your suffering? What risks can you take by setting the intention to "play" or have "fun?" What is your answer to "Why now?" and "What is the lesson here?"

CYNTHIA OLIVER

Gonna strike you down from your perch
There will be no ledge
No vantage
No church
Everything you've known will change
I'mma disorient ya
Take away what keeps you grounded, together, secure
What you thought would always be there
will crumble
And disappear
I'mma pull you out from your roots
Put ya where you can't grasp, can't reach
Ain't no fruit
I'mma make the earth shift

—CYNTHIA OLIVER, CHOREOGRAPHER
EXCERPTED BOOM! 2014

When Cynthia Oliver received an invitation to create an original dance piece in 2012, she wondered if her body would cooperate. It had been two years since she completed chemotherapy treatment for breast cancer. "I'd just come through this horrific experience. I didn't know if I was going to survive. I was really frightened." The invitation, which came from choreographer Bebe Miller, was to create an original dance piece for Ishmael Houston-Jones's Parallels in Black Platform Series at Danspace at St. Mark's Church in New York. When she told Bebe how vulnerable she felt at the thought of going back into the studio, Bebe replied, "Just try it."

After all, Cynthia had been making dances since 1991. Born in the Bronx, New York, and raised in the Virgin Islands, she cultivated a distinct choreographic and performative style reflecting the Caribbean performance and African and American aesthetic sensibilities that influenced her early development. In high school, she considered dance to be her hobby and visual arts her primary focus. Cynthia even took preparatory courses in architecture and engineering, thinking she might go in that direction. "But when recruiters came to my school and offered me the possibility of dance at a high level and with a scholarship, my hobby became my passion."

Since then, her work has been presented in New York, regionally and nationally. She is the recipient of many prestigious awards and recognitions as an artist and as a scholar, including a 2021 Doris Duke Award and as a 2022 MacDowell and Guggenheim Fellow. After earning her PhD in Performance Studies from New York University, she left New York in 2000 to join the University of Illinois at Urbana-Champaign as a professor in the dance department, where she served as the associate vice chancellor for research and innovation in the humanities, arts, and related fields.

Cynthia talked through her fears about Bebe's proposal to make a new dance piece with her longtime creative partner, composer, and husband, Jason Finkelman. He suggested perhaps finding a collaborator who would shift Cynthia's relationship to her fear about embarking on such a rigorous personal endeavor alone. Cynthia realized that what she wanted was someone who could give her permission "not to have to be boss lady."

She invited dance artist and performer Leslie Cuyjet to be her collaborator. "When I met her, she was a young college student who had that spark and a willingness to be uncertain and to try things." The synergy between them gave Cynthia the feeling of empowerment she needed to commit to a creative process. "I didn't want to feel the responsibility of being a leader and knowing all the answers. That shit can be exhausting. Leslie was someone I could be vulnerable with."

Even if Cynthia had no idea what would result from this collaboration, she trusted the creative process. "It is the making of work that allows me to process the experiences that I'm going through. So, in order for me to make sense of the world around me, I make dance theater works. It is a survival mechanism for me in the first place."

As her exploration progressed, she uncovered a belief she had formed as a child, which was "as a good Catholic girl, if you live life a particular way, a certain result is reasonable to expect."

She recalled a time when that belief was first challenged. As a young dancer/actor, she worked with award-winning writer, director, and performer Laurie Carlos on Carlos' award-winning play, *White Chocolate for My Father*. Laurie introduced Cynthia to a more experimental kind of performance, which challenged Cynthia's prior understanding of narrative structure in a play. "I had believed that there was a certain consciousness or spiritual progression that comes with one's lived experiences. Laurie disrupted that progression, and it changed my life then."

In one respect, her cancer diagnosis was, she says, "one of those things where, if you don't get the message fully the first time, life sort of circles back very choreographically and offers you an opportunity to get it a second time or third time or fourth time." Her cancer diagnosis offered a final stark liberation from the belief that her goodness would be enough to sustain the narrative continuity of her life. It was the moment she realized "life sort of laughed" at that belief and said, "'Well, I don't think so! How about *this*?'"

The process of fully integrating that message resulted in a new narrative. BOOM! was created in 2012 in collaboration with Leslie Cuyjet, just seventeen minutes in its first iteration. BOOM! was commissioned to be developed into a full evening, was presented in 2014, and toured for four years, longer than any of Cynthia's previous works.

Cynthia's decision to relinquish control of the direction of the piece allowed her to test other assumptions too. Her initial resistance to the invitation to "just try" was the belief she wouldn't have the physical strength to create the kind of work she knew in her heart this story demanded. "I was surprised at how much my body knew and could still accomplish. It took time, but it was there."

The supportive structure she built around the creation of this piece mitigated much of the fear she had about entering a process where she would be so vulnerable. "I think the scary part about it, and it's the same thing that I experience every time I walk into a studio to start a new work, is that I have not arrived at anything. There's nothing that I can count on to say, 'oh yeah, let me pull that out of my pocket, and I can do this thing.' I remember how."

She does have ways to get into creative flow, but there is no magic that can be used to alleviate what is scary about beginning again. "When I am at a loss in the studio, I will play a certain kind of music that strikes me that day, and it will at least get me moving. But it is not the thing that I settle on. It is rarely ever the thing that remains in the work."

Why did Cynthia create BOOM! and push further into a process of a transition so soon after her treatment ended? "Because that's why we're here," she says. "I really believe that's why we're here. We are meant to share that information. We're here for spiritual growth and consciousness development. That's why each of us has chosen to materialize in this earthly form."

It's not always an easy choice, but it does have its rewards. "I don't always like it twenty-four-seven. But there is some gratification in the practice, as hard as it is."

Cynthia acknowledges too that she is in the midst of a few other transitions right now. She just sent her son off to college, for one. And, in her early sixties, she is questioning the extent to which she moves away from her own personal dance practice. "I never thought I would get to the point in my life where I say to myself, 'I don't know if I have to dance today.' I don't know if I want to even do it for the next period of my life. I've done so much of it. My body is probably saying, 'Will you please just let me rest!'"

What she does know for sure is there will always be events, circumstances, and experiences that cause us to respond in different ways at different times. "There are multiple constellations operating all the time, constantly moving. Some are closer at certain times, and others recede." That kind of negotiation keeps us questioning, keeps us engaged, keeps us challenged. And it *is* challenging. I live for that."

BRAVING CREATIVITY

Once Cynthia chooses her collaborator, she dives headlong into the pillars of liberate, play, and empower in the creative process of making Boom! Even though the subject matter scares her, she is practiced at making dance theater work to process her life experiences. She trusts that inside a safe collaboration, she'll arrive at an empowered understanding of the transformation that has resulted from her crisis and recovery journey.

LIBERATE

It's important to emphasize Cynthia's observation that certain core beliefs operate in our unconscious mind as long as the underlying fear that fuels them remains in the dark. The crisis that was Cynthia's cancer diagnosis and treatment challenged a long-held unconscious belief that the path her life took in any way questioned her "goodness." She tested that assumption in a creative process that embodies her full and honest range of emotional experiences—the good, the bad, and the ugly. In essence, Cynthia exerts control over the narrative/spiritual progression of her story by writing and performing the truth of her experience and claims the indisputable goodness within that was always there.

PLAY AND EMPOWER

How often do we get an invitation to "just try" and immediately feel excitement and terror at the same time? Cynthia doubts her readiness to make a new work or explore such a vulnerable place in her heart alone in a creative process. She speaks to her husband, who reminds her that, first and foremost, she has options. Fear hates options. But our heart loves them. The suggestion of collaboration soothes Cynthia's fear long enough for her heart to explore the suggestion. Collaboration stimulates play and empowerment. With her trust in Leslie and with her years of experience making performance works behind her, Cynthia becomes empowered to enter the empty space she originally feared—not as boss lady or choreographer—but as a woman on a path of spiritual growth and consciousness development.

Cynthia constructs a new narrative with Boom!, which is its own story disruption. Boom! is a declaration that a new narrative can be written if we are willing to explore the truth in our shadow to express the goodness that is always already shining within us.

HOW DO YOU BRAVE CREATIVITY?

Have you received an invitation to "just try?" Who would you choose to accompany you into the empty space so you could brave creativity? Why do you think you are here in this earthly form?

ELJON WARDALLY

Even though it was a horrible, horrible thing that happened, something beautiful came out of it.

—ELJON WARDALLY, PLAYWRIGHT

In 2009, Eljon was working full-time in the beauty industry when she lifted a box in the mail room. "My neck was just burning, burning, burning, and then I got a huge headache." She went to the doctor several times. Even after one side of her body started to feel heavy and her foot was dragging a little, "the doctors continued to say 'It's just a migraine.'" They finally sent her for an MRI, and when she stepped off the train to go back to work after the test, the doctor called. "Can you get to the hospital on your own? You're having a stroke."

Eljon Wardally is an award-winning Grenadian and Italian American playwright and screenwriter who was born in New York and raised in the Italian neighborhood of Little Italy in Manhattan. She received her MFA in Playwriting from Fordham University as part of its inaugural playwriting class. With six one-act and seven full-length plays, she has received numerous awards and recognitions, including as a Signature Theater Launch Pad Residency Finalist, a Princess Grace playwriting Fellowship Finalist, and a four-time O'Neill National Playwrights' Conference finalist for her plays *Black Americanah for Sale*, *Blooming in Dry Season*, and *Big Black Balloon*. Most recently, she is the recipient of the "Finding

Holy Ground" Playwriting Commission from Wake Forest University, North Carolina Black Rep, and Wake the Arts.

Eljon grew up as an only child and knew early on she was an artist. "I was my own playmate. I created stories and worlds with my toys." Growing up in downtown Manhattan in the 1980s and early 1990s, she was exposed to art and artists. "I was surrounded by creative people and creativity." The blocks surrounding her apartment were a favorite location for film productions. "I thought I wanted to be an actor. I'd hang out on my block where *Law and Order* would be filming. My mom would say, 'If I can see you from the window, you can go out and talk with them.'" Eljon wasn't shy about asking questions of the production staff she met on the street. "I got a lot of information that way. I really thought I was going to be an actor."

In high school, she joined Downtown Art, a theater on Fourth Street. "I found myself more interested in character from a writing standpoint and storytelling from a writer standpoint than in acting." While she was there, she tested her playwriting chops. "I wrote little scenes and little sketches, but I wouldn't really share them with anybody." Slowly, she began to realize, "Oh, I can be a writer." But that kind of training wasn't offered in her school. "I went to Catholic school on my street. We didn't have theater. We didn't have dance. We didn't have access to any of that stuff." Instead of dropping her interest in writing, Eljon took advantage of the art going on in her neighborhood. "I thought, *Okay, this thing is happening on the street. That will be where my education comes from.*"

Eljon's parents weren't artists and didn't know how to guide her career. "My mom was a first-grade teacher. She didn't have her finger on the pulse of artistic things going on. And my dad was a contractor from Grenada, so he had no idea." When she arrived at Clark University as a freshman, there wasn't even a playwriting class. She took acting classes, and to keep writing, she wrote short films with her friends outside of class. She submitted her work to two festivals thinking, she says, "I'm just going to throw it against the wall, see if it sticks. And it did." In one year, she had two one-act plays, *The Gift*, which was accepted into The Network One Act Festival at the Barrow Group, and *Home Sweet Home*, which was accepted into One Act Festival and into the Strawberry Festival at the Riant Theater, both in New York. When those plays came to fruition, Eljon thought, *Maybe this can actually be something*. Still, she kept her excitement to herself. "I guess I was half-assed doing it." Right after that, she had a stroke. She was twenty-nine years old.

The doctor's phone call and diagnosis didn't register at first. "When I hung up the phone, I was actually laughing. It didn't sink in." On her way from the subway to the emergency room, she said, "I texted my boyfriend and said, 'Hey, so I can't hang out later. I'm having a stroke. I'll probably be home by dinner.' I told my mom, 'Don't panic, I'm having a stroke. I'm going to the hospital. Don't worry about it. I'll be fine. You don't even have to leave work.'" Eljon got in a cab, and when she tried to pay the cab driver, her hands couldn't complete the transaction. It took about twenty-four hours before she realized she was in the stroke unit of an intensive care unit.

After two days in the ICU, she was stable enough to move into the general stroke care unit. "I just wanted to get out of there." To keep her there, she said, "My mom took my wallet and my shoes and said, 'Now how are you going to leave? You have no money, and you have no shoes. And it's November. You're staying here.'"

As Eljon looked around the hospital room, she finally understood the severity of her diagnosis. "The person next to me thinks it's 1973. And the person across from me is unconscious. I'm the youngest person here. And I'm the only person who knows what day and time it is."

When she got home, Eljon felt euphoric for a while. She minimized her fear, telling herself, "Everything's fine. If I don't wake up, cool." She started giving away things, "like, here, take this, it's fine."

Once the euphoria subsided, panic set in and she had trouble sleeping. "I couldn't go to sleep because I thought that I might not wake up," she recalled. Her anxiety expanded into other areas of her life. "I felt like I was in a movie where the stakes are rising and you are anticipating that something much worse is going to happen."

Just three months after she was released from the hospital, while watching an episode of *Law and Order*, she had an idea. "I just started to write." She got excited about a previous fascination with the untold stories of characters from crime dramas. "When I'm watching any show, I want to know what happens to the family after the verdict is announced. I want to know *that* story. So I wrote a scene, and I sent it to my boyfriend." Eljon's boyfriend Randy is a director, and she was nervous about his feedback. She was worried that maybe her writing suffered from the stroke. She recalled him saying, "This is actually really good. We should make it into a short film." They made the short film in that same year, and it ended up getting into over forty-five festivals worldwide. "And from there, we created a web series based off the first thing that I wrote after my stroke."

Once her speech and memory had improved enough, she decided to "listen to the Universe and apply to grad school and pursue playwriting full steam ahead." She was one of two candidates accepted into the inaugural playwriting MFA class at Fordham University. "The stroke kind of kicked me into high gear."

Applying for a playwriting degree was one triumph, but there was still more in this transition for her to grapple with. Eljon's blood thinners were having a devastating effect on her mental health. "My complexion was gray. I have curly hair, and my curls were turning to waves. It felt like I had transformed from the inside out, and not in a great way. When I looked in the mirror I had to ask, who is this?"

After taking her final medication, in a symbolic gesture of reclamation, she cut off her hair. "I got a faux hawk." But that also meant letting go of a part of who she was, which was scary. "My mom kept my hair very, very, very short until I was twelve." As a kid, Eljon wanted to grow her hair out, but she said, "My mom would never listen to me because she didn't know how to do my hair, nor did she ever take the time to learn how to do it." Eljon said cutting it herself was liberating, "It was the start of taking control back."

Having come so close to losing so much, she said, "I'm trying to be comfortable with not knowing what's ahead. It's a constant effort for me to surrender. I can't manipulate time. I can't make it move faster or slower. Time moves how it moves. I just have to be okay with what's happening."

This mix of control, grief, and time is so poignant for Eljon. "I'm writing something about three sisters who live together in a boat on top of a hill. There is no water around. Their dad built the boat because he is afraid that God is going to destroy the world by flooding it again. So, if that happens, they will be ready because they're in this boat. But they're terrified to leave. Eventually, the father dies, and they still don't leave their boat because they believe that if they do, something bad is going to happen." Eljon takes one small step at a time so she can mitigate the big fears she has about unknown dangers, like flying in an airplane, for instance, by reminding herself that she can't live her life afraid of what might happen in the future.

Last year, Eljon had a bad sinus infection that knocked out much of her sense of smell and taste. "My morning practice would have been to have a cup of coffee or a cup of tea, hold the cup close to my nose, and take it in. Now, I'm looking out at the clouds and looking at the buildings. I'm looking at the people and being grateful for being able to start the day."

BRAVING CREATIVITY

Eljon's childhood determination to navigate herself toward playwriting gets supercharged once she liberates herself from her fears. The stroke empowers her to claim her belonging and identity as an artist and playwright in a big way.

LIBERATE AND NAVIGATE

One step forward and two steps back; that is Eljon's dance throughout high school and college. Her ambivalence about committing to herself as a playwright is also a necessary primer. It readies her to take bigger and bigger risks as she inches closer to who she will ultimately become.

Underneath Eljon's self-declared "half-assed" effort at playwriting is a fear-fueled belief. Maybe she is afraid of succeeding; maybe she is afraid of being seen as an impostor without "formal" training; maybe she is afraid of failure. All those fears make sense, and we've all felt them when we stop short of committing to our big vision.

The stroke threatens the very thing Eljon has secretly wished for since middle school, and it also catalyzes her passionate pursuit of it. Barely in recovery for three months, Eljon has the idea for her short film. She proceeds to write at a time when her memory and speech are impaired, when she is anxious and worried about her future, when she has no certainty at all about the work being any good. That is when she has the courage to take a brave step forward and commit to going "full steam" ahead.

EMPOWER

Eljon takes back her narrative from the one her stroke could have written for her when she decides to follow the wisdom of the Universe that has declared: *Now is the time.* She now feels entitled to pursue the direction her heart has been pointing her toward for so long. Less afraid of what she doesn't know and can't control, she is grateful for the present moment. With this mindset, she focuses on what she *can* control—her presence, her beauty, and a trust in something larger that holds it all.

HOW DO YOU BRAVE CREATIVITY?
What is your heart navigating you toward? When you listen to the Universe, what does it say? What do you want to pursue "full steam ahead?" What are you grateful for?

MADDIE CORMAN

You can't express grief in a scientific way.
It's like you need Mary Oliver,
you need somebody splattering paint,
you need an actress screaming
and having, you know, snot running down their nose.
MADDIE CORMAN, ACTRESS AND WRITER

In the summer of 2015, actress Maddie Corman was on a sound stage in Brooklyn filming a guest spot on a popular television show when she received a phone call. Her husband of eighteen years was being arrested. Her daughter and younger twin boys were home when the police came for him.

Corman's private life was suddenly made jarringly public. She grasped for reassurance that there would be a way to endure all the emotions that were unleashed inside of her with this event. "When my life blew up, one of the ways I tried to put it back together was finding books or artwork, or podcasts, or plays, or anything that I could see myself in because it was an extremely lonely time. I felt like no one else had ever felt the way I felt."

With a thirty-year career in theater, television, and film, Maddie is most well-known by her peers for her role in John Hughes' *Some Kind of Wonderful* and for originating the role of Holly in the Tony-nominated production of Geoffrey'

Nauffts' *Next Fall*, which went to Broadway. Six months after her husband's arrest, she started to write the work that would result in her first one-woman play *Accidentally Brave*.

When Maddie was in high school, she thought of herself as a writer. "I loved writing. I was good at it." As a freshman year English major in college, she applied for a creative writing course with a formidable and famous teacher who required the approval of a writing sample to gain admittance. Maddie didn't get in. "I was embarrassed and upset. And honestly, a teeny bit devastated. I never took another writing class."

Shortly after that first shocking phone call, Maddie received a call from a woman she calls "My Angel." Maddie refers to her Angel in *Accidentally Brave* as a woman who is "very amazing and very famous, and I have never met her and we have almost no friends in common' . . . and before I go any further, no, I am not going to tell you who she is" (Corman 2021, 17). Based on her Angel's own life experience, she wanted to help guide and comfort Maddie. "She helped me beyond words. She shared her own story, which was different from mine in the details, but a lot of the feelings were really similar. And whereas so many people around me, including people I love very much, would say, 'I can't even imagine,' she never said that. She said, 'I can absolutely imagine, and here I am. And here's my story.' And that was incredibly comforting to me." At some point during that first year, Maddie asked her Angel how she could ever repay her for her companionship and counsel during so many painful and confusing moments after the arrest. "And she said, 'Just pay it forward.' Although I don't think she meant go ahead and write a solo off-Broadway show."

Maddie started acting when she was six years old. She understood the extent to which outside validation sated an unconscious anxiety about her own worth. That one early experience of rejection from a college writing class caused her to doubt her writing ability. "I so badly didn't want to be bad at something." But about a year after her husband's arrest, Maddie started to feel an urgency to write. "I did feel an actual burning desire inside to share the messy part. I knew to do that was to write the truth of it. I still didn't know how I was going to express that."

Maddie has spent her career working in ensemble casts. She had never written or performed a solo show, and that wasn't what she set out to do. "There was something about this story that required me to be alone to tell it, because it was the loneliest time in my life." Maddie grappled with many complex thoughts and emotions that she wanted to explore in words, and she knew any process of creative exploration would require some emotional and creative support. "It was important to me to have a safe person by my side to run things by as I was writing. Someone I could turn to and say, 'No, I don't want to include that,' 'Yes, I can include that,' 'Wait, maybe I can say this in a way that is from my point of view.'"

She chose theater director Kristin Hanggi. "I'd been working in the entertainment industry for years. I mean many, many, many years. And I knew many, many, many people. But there was something about Kristin that felt right. And not to get all woo-woo, but there was something woo-woo in there. I reached out to her one day, and she answered, 'Oh yes, I've been waiting for your call,' which, if you know Kristin, isn't that crazy."

"I wasn't interested in having conversations that didn't involve real life and what was really going on, but it was also too much to have lunch with people and talk about the weather." So, instead, she got down to the business of writing. Maddie set out to mine her memory to make sense of her own personal experience of that time. "I worked in a womb-like setting with Kristin for months. And at some point, it became clear that it was a monologue. It wasn't a TED Talk, it wasn't really a Moth piece, it wasn't going to be a play with different cast members in it, it wasn't going to be a book or a short story."

She knew she had to use a medium where she could communicate beyond words about the depth of her experience. "You know, the sound that I made when I was lying on the bathroom floor, it was guttural and animalistic, and I didn't want to just talk about it, I wanted to show it." But making decisions about the content for this story was hard. "It was important to me to tell the story. And yet, it's a true story. And it involves other people. I was, and am, very aware of my children and what they might think and what they might want to be told. And at the same time, I did not and do not know how to tell this story without the angle of motherhood. It *is* the story. It is my story in so many ways."

At that point, Kristin suggested to Maddie that now might be the time to find a rehearsal space. "And I was like, 'Oh God, no.' And then I thought, *Okay, I'm gonna listen. I'm gonna listen my intuition.* Kristin is just so mystical, and she said, 'Just close your eyes. Where do you see it?'"

Everything went very quickly from there. "A week later, I was in a rehearsal room in a theater." By the end of that week,

Maddie was offered space in a winter reading series by the theater's director. "And I said absolutely not. And then the next day, it was like, well, okay." Maddie had never read the piece out loud to anyone before. "I invited about sixteen people and stood on a stage with a music stand and said the words out loud for the first time. I learned that night that this was a play. I also learned the power of telling this story for an audience and for myself. I felt it as healing, even in my terror."

That reading gave her the feedback she needed to continue to develop and workshop the piece twice more. "I was always an actor for hire. Suddenly, I was driving the car." For the third reading, Maddie reached out to producer Daryl Roth, who gifted Maddie her theater for a day. "We picked a date that I knew [Daryl] would be there, and I invited a bunch of other people. By that point, we had really honed the piece. It was still just me and a music stand and an audience, a full house."

Within twenty-four hours of that reading, Daryl asked Maddie if she could produce her show. Suddenly, Maddie had resources and people she could bring into her creative process. "To creatively collaborate on something I had in my head and then bring it to a team was really exciting and much less lonely."

When they finally began to perform the show, Maddie realized she would have to find a sustainable performance strategy. "I couldn't actually relive that story eight times a week or I would die. So how much of my actual acting technique could I use?" She understood that, although this was her personal story, it was being presented as a piece of art. "It didn't change night to night. I had a costume." When her kids would come with her husband to pick her up from the theater, she said,

"I'd say, 'Just give me a minute, I have to change' and they'd say, 'What do you mean you're changing? You're just playing yourself.' And I'd remind them, 'No, I have a costume and I have a microphone. It's not just me making it up.'"

It was around this time that Maddie really started to trust her writing. "There is a part of me that believes as an actor, you serve your writer, you serve your playwright, your screenwriter, your television writer, and that's your job. I came up as a theater performer. So it's really 'The playwright is God.' But suddenly, I was the playwright."

"It's really scary to rely on myself." It took her time to trust the quality of her writing. "I trusted myself more as an actor than a writer. But as I went along, I would have times where I would just work on one scene or one section, and I'd think, *Oh, this is good.*" It's still hard for her to hear herself say that. "I needed to trust that I had created something solid and to trust that one day, someone else could play the part, that it's not just about me standing and talking. It's about the fact that I created a piece."

By then, Maddie understood *Accidentally Brave* was an exploration of not only of her own private feelings but feelings that might be relatable to anyone who had experienced their own major crisis. "I think in good art, and I hope that people might think this is good art, you see humanity and you see nuance in situations where you might not have before. It's easy to judge, but it's not as easy to judge when you see yourself in the artwork. I think the more specific I allowed myself to get, the more the audience responded by recognizing that they had those same feelings even in the most different scenarios."

After the show, Maddie met audience members in the lobby. She called it the "second act." "It really became a confessional of sorts, where people, night after night, would tell me their stories. There was a young man one night whose sister died in a car accident. And he said, 'You know, I had that moment of thinking my life was one thing. And then in one moment, everything changed. And, like you, I also wondered, would we ever laugh again? And then we laughed. And it was like, wait, are we allowed to laugh?' Different gender, different relationship, different circumstances, but the humanity of the feelings that go with a trauma can be universal."

In order to anchor herself in the details of the experience, which were still incomprehensible, she had to get very quiet. "I didn't grab my journal and think, *Let me write down the adorable thing my daughter said while we were all freaking out.* I didn't do that." Without a linear accounting to refer to, Maddie leaned on her devices. "When I did decide I wanted to write, I did go back to look at my calendar. I did go back and look at texts to friends and to my husband."

Maddie wanted to communicate the spiritual aspect of surrendering to something bigger than ourselves in order to endure the extreme uncertainty the upheaval caused. "I was looking at a person I love who had to surrender to the law. But I also had to surrender [to something]." And in her surrender, Maddie gave herself over to the fact that, "Yes, it's unmanageable. And I can't figure this out."

That kind of surrender was not totally unfamiliar to Maddie. Her mother died when she was about the same age as her daughter was when her husband was arrested. "There's something about grief and trauma where I'm like, I'm going to be really mature and really grown up, and I'm going to hold on really tight, and you're not going to see me lose control. But losing control is part of the creative process and part of the fun of life."

In a way, creating this piece helped Maddie claim space as an artist. "I shudder at even calling myself an artist, but it is a part of who I am. And that's how I process things." So, when she wanted to make sense of this crisis, she used her artistry. "This is the way I know how to do that. It made a little bit of sense to me. It's not like I was a carpenter. So even though I didn't know I *could* do it, there was a part of me that trusted that this was the way to process this experience."

Maddie said it was a kind of faith she had in herself that helped her move forward even when she didn't know what would happen next. "It's not that I stopped being afraid. I just invited that fear to standby next to me. But sometimes in my body, fear seemed to feel really similar to excitement. And so I just had to keep remembering that maybe I'm also excited."

"If I could have kept my husband's arrest a secret, I probably would have, except it was in the fucking *New York Post*. That's why my story is called *Accidentally Brave*, because it's not that brave. And I don't know that I would have been brave enough to do it otherwise." But she said giving a voice to her experience has made an impact that has fueled her courage to continue with her work. "I have a bit of a mission, and no matter how battered I get, I will continue because I know there are people who've experienced the show, who say 'Thank you. I needed to hear that.'"

Accidentally Brave is now a published play with an Audible version. A film of the production was executive produced by Steven Soderbergh and is currently in post-production. When I asked Maddie if she considers herself a writer now that her play has had such success, she said, "I mean, what time is it today, this is Thursday? I do. Today, I am excited to continue to write. I am. And I also now really appreciate when someone else just hands me something."

BRAVING CREATIVITY

Liberate, navigate, and empower create the most radical shifts in Maddie's transition story. Maddie relies on her intuition to take her first brave steps into the unknown after her crisis. She discovers a new belief about herself as an artist and a writer and puts what she discovers into a newfound mission for her life.

LIBERATE

Maddie's crisis is the catalyst for her liberation from the fear of being bad. The feeling that her rejection from a college writing course touched upon was shame. "I am bad." Her interpretation of the rejection was a belief that "I am a bad writer because I was not accepted into this class." And it hurt so much that she didn't want to do the thing (writing) that invited that feeling (shame) ever again. So she made a commitment to not do the writing that she loved because she now believed she was bad at it. The crisis creates a crack in that belief and releases a deep knowing that reveals itself as a burning desire to write.

NAVIGATE

Maddie must navigate with her heart because her thinking mind is offline after the crisis. She is open to her intuition and can receive guidance from her "Angel" and from Kristin, her writing partner. As her outer resources strengthen her inner knowing, she can trust the intuition that arises that tells her it's time to move from Kristin's apartment to a rehearsal space. The ability to welcome fear and excitement at the same time is such a wonderful insight because it shows us how we must learn to hold both in order to brave creativity and create new meaning and purpose in our lives.

EMPOWERED

Maddie now feels empowered to be on the stage with this story. Once her fear is in plain sight, she can walk with it right up to center stage and call it excitement. As her sense of entitlement to her story grows, people respond, her story resonates, and the project grows. Out of this time, too, comes a clarity of purpose she calls her mission. Maddie is on her way to flourishing by the end of this story because she has practiced surrendering to something bigger than her fear of being bad.

HOW DO YOU BRAVE CREATIVITY?

What feels scary to you now, but also kind of exciting? Have you received guidance from your heart in a whisper? Is there something you know you are great at, and love, but don't do because of something someone said once?

SARA JULI

There are many, many days
when I would like to not do this work.
It's time-consuming, it's costly, and it's really hard,
vulnerable, and painful on many levels.
But I just have to do it, because this is how
I make sense of the world.
I can see it as odd, but then
I can also see it as beautiful and necessary.

—SARA JULI, PERFORMANCE ARTIST

When Sara Juli was invited to restage her solo performance piece *Burnt-Out Wife* at the South Miami-Dade Cultural Arts Center in Miami, Florida in 2021, much of what had inspired the creation of the piece had changed. She created *Burnt-Out Wife* in 2018-19 at a time when her two children had become independent enough for her to turn her attention toward her marriage. "I was able to ask, what didn't get tended to while I was mothering and surviving and working and making peanut butter and jelly sandwiches? My marriage. And I saw it as an absolute mess."

Sara has been performing personal stories using dance, comedy, and theatrical elements for over two decades. She said she makes work in order to make sense of her world, creating a body of work that deals with everything from death to sex to money and marriage. "The topics that I make work about run concurrently with my life. The dances I was creating in my twenties are different from my thirties, which are different from my forties."

Sara began solo performance work in 2000 and has performed at notable venues in New York City, regionally and internationally. In 2006, at the age of twenty-seven, she created and performed her first full-evening solo show *The Money Conversation*. To reassess her relationship to money, during the performance, she offered her entire life's savings of $5,000 at the time to the audience as she moved from the stage to the risers, inviting them to extract bills stashed under her clothes, in proximity to her private parts. In 2015, she created and performed *Tense Vagina: an actual diagnosis* using humor, text, music, and physical interaction with the audience to raise awareness on topics related to women's birthing experiences, which are still considered taboo to discuss openly, like postpartum depression and post-childbirth urinary incontinence.

Her motivation to tell her stories is two-fold, she said. "It originates from a place of wanting to help myself navigate the planet and make sense of my world." And the second reason Sara tackles such personal subjects "is the drive to have these topics help others heal." She describes further, "These are complex issues, and they are felt by millions of people at any given time. So that's always been my inspiration for working with such difficult material, connecting to the pain we all feel, and connecting that pain to each other."

In 2017, her marriage became the thing that didn't make sense. The emotions that drove the creation of *Burnt-Out Wife* were primarily anger and blame. "I pointed my finger at my partner and was like, *You're* the problem! And I started a creative process from that space, which is really quite toxic." Making work that, as Sara said, "is filled with anger and rage and finger-pointing" was reinforcing a path toward the dissolution of their marriage. "To use the 'D word,' I felt that we were headed in that direction, which is a culturally taboo and a difficult word to say, still. But that's where I felt that we were."

Having made *Burnt-Out Wife*, it wasn't lost on Sara that she had attached her identity to certain fairy-tale tropes, which reinforced the narrative that it was her husband who was failing to follow the script. However, there was a part of her that sensed she played a part too. "I do recall in the process of making the piece prior to therapy, thinking, *Wait a minute. Throwing him under the bus so easily? That can't be fully right.*" Completing *Burnt-Out Wife* signaled a turning point in the relationship. "It was like, 'Okay, are we going down the divorce path, or do we do want to stay together?' And I definitely remember feeling that I had an equal responsibility to do the work. But I didn't know quite what it was that I'd have to work *through*."

The set for *Burnt-Out Wife* was a bathroom painted a Pepto-Bismol pink and everything contained within—a tub and shower, toilet, and plunger—were the same color. During a dance sequence set to the sound of a man urinating, Sara dances in a robe affixed with tampons and sanitary pads, made by her longtime costume designer Carol Farrell. She fed the audience chocolate bundt cake by hand and asked them "What if" questions. "What if we were married, but we lived in separate houses across the street from each other?

What do you think?" "What if we were married, and every year, we got to have an affair with someone else? What do you think?" "What if we were married to different people, but every three months, we got together and had sex? What do you think?"

Burnt-Out Wife was scheduled for a national tour that had been two years in the making when the pandemic shut the tour down. Of the pandemic time, she said, "We were suddenly homebound, and it felt like we had a choice: go our separate ways or dig in and do the work." For Sara, that choice to go to marriage counseling and into her own deep therapeutic work "has been nothing short of transformational, nothing short of risky, and nothing short of lifesaving. Doing that weekly work together, I saw how much I was complicit in and an equal contributor in the mess that I perceived. In truth, we had created it together."

Sara and her husband spent two years working intensively with a marriage counselor—and still going strong in continuing that work. So, when she was invited to perform the piece again in August 2021, she thought, "*This piece is a representation of a* past self *who's gone through this journey. And in a way, I was embarrassed by parts of the piece where I really was pointing a finger at my partner.* I ended up altering the piece in minor but important ways." Sara still sees the value in honoring that time and those feelings that were alive then in the work. "I have changed the ending. And I have added more text about taking responsibility for my part. I've kept the anger and the finger-pointing in the piece, intentionally as an homage or as an honoring of the reality that was real at the time. And I do something called acting. That's a thing."

Sara said her husband attended the pre-pandemic openings for *Burnt-Out Wife* and "loved it for its aesthetic and bravery." However, when Sara performs the show now, they agree that he doesn't continue to attend. "While he can separate fact from fiction, the comments he hears from other people—yes, mostly negative toward him—before, during, and after the show can be challenging. It can be painful for him to be there, especially when people make assumptions about him, and then too painful for me to perform knowing what he's dealing with."

Making this work and performing it allowed Sara to release the defensive narratives that kept her from tending to those parts of herself that wanted her version of a storybook marriage. "Doing the work of marriage is letting go of all of those ideas and living in the present equally with your partner." The arc of Sara's transition process between the pandemic and returning to tour has been one healing journey. "The truth is that our partner is the most important person in our lives, and this work has helped me understand how to honor that truth in healthy ways, both for my partner and for myself."

Another crucial insight that arose from her work on *Burnt-Out Wife* and in her private therapeutic work was a belief that was holding so much anger and resentment for Sara, but it had eluded her early in her creative process. "It's half-ridiculous. It's a crying little girl who is holding on to the eight-year-old savior fantasy of, you know, pick your trope: Damsel in Distress? Cinderella? Lois Lane? It's like a rom-com narrative that, as a little girl, I held onto as the ideal but is far from anything real or even desirable." Under that belief, she realized, was something that would take her deeper into the unknown. "It was finally time to touch the untouchable."

In late September 2022, Sara presented twenty minutes of a work in progress showing of *Naughty* at the Strand Theatre in Rockland, Maine. This piece brings her into direct contact with that same eight-year-old self who was molested as a child. Sara approached the showing like she had approached the hundred other showings she had done of previous works, but this one wasn't like the others. "While I was performing, I felt like I had to stop and cry numerous times. And then we had a post-performance discussion. I've done a million post-performance discussions in my career, and yet I was grossly underprepared to be on a microphone talking about my sexual trauma to a roomful of strangers for forty minutes."

Sara started to feel nauseous about thirty minutes into the showing. She realized after she made it through the showing that "I needed to take a breather or should have asked for a shorter post-performance discussion or have protected myself better." The showing took a toll on her over the next few days. "My body was having a different response than my mind was having, and I didn't quite fully have a handle on the emotional impact of working through my trauma in performance yet." That will be the work of this next year of development.

She learned from the work-in-progress showing that "I don't have to perform the trauma to make a strong piece of art that will resonate with audiences." But to explore the full arc of the experience, it will take as much time as her creative processes requires. "I need at least two years. The development of good art over time is its own thing. And then working through trauma over time is a totally separate task. And then I lay them on top of each other. I know I can do this, but I just need a lot of space to work through this."

"As daunting as it is to work on this new piece, there is an excitement about the growth that can come from the process. That's a gift to the little girl inside me. It says to her, 'I still believe in my worth, I still believe that I'm whole, I still believe I have something to say.'"

But she also has a job to do. "A woman came up to me at the *Naughty* showing. She was in her twenties. She said, 'What you did was incredibly meaningful. I was molested when I was four, and I've been working through that trauma. Thank you, thank you.' When she walked away, I said to myself, 'That's it. Everything was for this person.'"

That time in front of the audience is the payoff for the risk Sara takes to put such personal material on stage. "It's euphoric." Working with choreographer Deborah Hay early in her career taught her the value of harnessing that euphoria and transforming it into care. "There's nothing like it. It's the greatest gift I could ever give myself and give my children and give those who come to see my shows. To say, 'I know how to handle you. And I know how to handle your anger because I have that anger too. Let's work together in this space and find the soft and find the settling and find the humor.' That's why I love performing so much."

One of Sara's most powerful relational performance skills is her use of comedy. She knows it will take time to find the humor in *Naughty*. "I really want to find the comedy. We could all sit in this room and cry together, because that's how much pain we're all in at any given moment. But let's use it productively instead. Let's laugh a little. Yes, we can cry a little if we want. But let's do some work together instead. Let's move something that's holding us back in our minds just an inch forward. If one person watches *Burnt-Out Wife* and says, 'Hmm, I need to think a little bit more about my relationship with my partner,' then I have done my job."

BRAVING CREATIVITY

In Sara's story, we can see how it is possible to carry certain beliefs with us for a lifetime without being pressed to challenge them at the deepest level. A looming crisis, like the end of a marriage, is the catalyst for a crack to form in the foundation of a belief that was set early in Sara's life because of her childhood trauma.

LIBERATE

Sometimes our own truth is so obscured by the fear stitched inside of our wounds that the only way to find out what is possible beyond our suffering is to walk right toward it, open it up, and look inside. Sara created *Burnt-Out Wife* to dive into the dilemma of her marriage. But it was not until she was quarantined at home during the COVID pandemic that she confronted the choice she must make.

Sara chooses to explore underneath her anger and blame. What she found there was the inconsolable grief of a much younger part of her that was carrying the hope that someone would rescue her. Sara liberates herself when she goes toward the ultimate darkness and grapples with the creative process of making her newest piece, *Naughty*.

NAVIGATE

Sara entered the creation of *Burnt-Out Wife* to help herself make sense of and navigate a world where threat was present. At first, the threat seemed to be the end of her marriage. Sensing that "something isn't right here" was a message from her heart to go deeper into the wound causing the disruption she was experiencing in her life.

Sara describes a moment when she recognizes conflicting messages coming from her mind and body during the work-in-progress showing of *Naughty*. This is a great example of how our mind so deftly interferes with our receptivity. Even when Sara feels resistance in her body—when she feels nausea and the sting of tears rising—her mind marshals thoughts to shut down the threat it perceives, which is her vulnerability. It is this dance between liberation and navigation that Sara has committed to pursuing in her work and life that makes it possible for her to create enough safety inside herself to inch forward in her transition process toward her most courageous self-expression yet.

EMPOWERED

Like Maddie, Sara uses humor to connect to the audience on an energetic level so she can communicate what can't be felt in words. And like Maddie too, she speaks about the connection to the audience as part of her own healing work that compels her to continue to give voice to the most difficult narratives in her life. It is in the relationship to an audience that they both learn to trust the gift in this expression and claim their right to tell their stories.

HOW DO YOU BRAVE CREATIVITY?

What about your behavior confuses you? Can you get curious about what causes the confusion? When you feel blame, can you investigate what hurt is there?

GRIEF

*In order to create, we have to stand in that space between
what we see in the world and
what we hope for looking squarely at rejection,
at heartbreak, at war, at death.
That's a tough space to stand in.*

—JULIE BERNSTEIN

*We often believe that our grief will grow smaller in time.
It doesn't.
We must grow bigger.*

—DAVID KESSLER

I keep a small ceramic heart in my pocket. One summer Saturday morning, I carried this thin little heart, the size of a silver dollar, in my pocket to the farmers' market. My kids, eleven and eight then, were running around with friends, jacked up on lemonade and pastries. I stood behind the crowd, looking at young couples and their small children who were seated at the few scattered picnic tables or on blankets listening to a single musician strum a guitar at the center of the lawn. I couldn't bear it. I couldn't bear anything about it.

I was clearly resisting my new reality. As my heart shredded inside my chest, I held the small heart in my pocket so tightly I thought it would snap in half. I pressed my thumb and pointer finger into its smooth red glaze. I was bracing in the face of extreme grief, trying to resist feeling the whole of it. The happy scene I was observing in front of me challenged my belief that this was supposed to be my life too. *I should be sitting on the lawn or walking my dog through the farmers' market with my healthy husband.* But instead, I was grasping this little heart in my pocket and releasing that belief one painful swallow at a time.

Around the same time, I met a painter about my age whose husband had died suddenly a week before mine. For several years, we met with a group of fifty other grieving families in a bereavement group. Parents assembled in small rooms packed with couches, our children sorted into their own groups by age. During our first year-end ceremony, the children presented pillows they had made with photos of the parent who died printed on the fabric and embellished with craft glitter, markers, and gems. After the pillow ceremony, we assembled for our regular closing ritual by forming an oval-shaped ring with our hands clasped. We filled out the perimeter of the school-sized cafeteria. My friend, who is at least four inches taller, leaned over me. Her big blue eyes widened, and her smile spread as she sang in a whisper,

"Are you k-i-i-i-ding? You mean we have to do this for-e-e-e-ver? It's so horrible."

Like me, my friend felt how impossible it was to hold both extreme grief and love at the same time without breaking under the weight of it. Just like the message in her whisper, the expectation that we could seemed so absurd it was almost laughable. But it is precisely the tension in that paradox that gives it its creative power and reveals our shared humanity in the moments when we struggle to hold both.

Grief is part of our everyday life. It's under every sudden hurt, every irritation, and every burst of anger. But when given a choice, we'd often rather skip over grief, favoring stability over the gap that opens when an uncomfortable feeling is present. Why? Tami Simon, founder of Sounds True and author of *Being True*, says the reason we don't tolerate that level of truth in those moments is because "We're terrified. We're all terrified. The gap is terrifying" (Simon 2016, 8:30).

To avoid feeling the grief concealed inside of our longing, we ignore, we deny, we distract, we blame, we judge, we manipulate, and we make assumptions. I spent two years before my husband died hardly shedding a tear for fear of what might erupt if I allowed myself to feel anything at all.

I had an experience days after Eric's funeral. In a single moment, standing at the threshold between the living room and the front door, I felt overcome by love. I felt the immensity of all of the love I had, which felt like all of the love in the world. Instead of experiencing less love as a result of my loss, I was able to feel all the love there was, and it was so big, bigger than I had ever felt love before.

The quality of time in grief is not the same as we experience on other days. The challenge with all transition is allowing ourselves time to hang out in that void, without leaping, skipping over, or turning back. My grief counselor said, "Try to let the Universe fill that empty space. Don't interfere with it by trying to fill it yourself. Just let it do its part and see what happens."

In the stories that follow, see if you can observe moments when the artists hold the tension of grief and love, when they explore the scary gaps and trust the Universe to fill the void. The artists in this section help us explore how grief transforms our experience of love and also of time. In Julia Mandle's story, she communes with extreme grief and extreme beauty as a result of her time spent in the void left by her father's death. Playwright L M Feldman uses Instagram to mark the passage of time after the breakup of her longtime relationship. And Chie Fueki begins a series of paintings during the COVID pandemic that reflect the feeling of transience she has felt since kindergarten.

JULIA MANDLE

Never rush your mourning process,
take your time for it because in mourning
there is so much important information.
—JULIA MANDLE, MULTIMEDIA ARTIST

Julia Mandle sits on the floor of her studio in Amsterdam in front of a giant canvas splattered with black paint. She speaks as if she's reciting a poem, with deliberate gentle pacing. A tattoo of an arrow snakes around her forearm. "The biggest change recently is the loss of my father."

Julia began her career as a conceptual artist and performance art creator in New York in the late 1990s/early 2000s. While in New York, she established a nonprofit, J Mandle Performance, that presented large-scale, site-specific performances and installations at venues, including the New Museum of Contemporary Art, Cooper Hewitt National Design Museum, the Highline, Storefront for Art & Architecture, Van Allen Institute, and The Old American Can Factory. Julia is a graduate of Williams College with an MFA from the Gallatin School at New York University. She is recipient of a New York Foundation for the Arts Fellowship and has received support from the National Endowment for the Arts, The Foundation for Contemporary Art, from the Amsterdam Fund for the Arts (AFK), and the Mondriaan Fund. She has been an artist resident at Yaddo, Baryshnikov Arts

Center, Guapamacataro Mexico, Weir Farm Trust, and most recently at European Ceramic Work Center (EKWC) in the Netherlands.

Julia's lens for seeing the world is the result of her upbringing. Her mother, Gayle Wells Mandle, is a mixed media artist and painter. Her father, Roger Mandle, started out as a painter and then studied art history and museum administration. He became a leading arts administrator at the National Gallery in Washington, DC, and then president of the Rhode Island School of Design (RISD).

Julia said of spending time at the National Gallery with her father, "One of my favorite things as a child was to walk through the museum where he worked. We would hold hands, and he would bring me into the room and say, 'Well, if you could have any painting in this room, what would it be?' And then he would use his hands to gesture about the composition's shadow and how the artist laid down a stroke of paint and created texture. And I felt like 'Oh my God, I was right there with Rembrandt.'"

On her last visit to America before the pandemic, they stopped by the ocean as they always did on their way to the airport. "I made a photographic image of him stretching his arms out wide with his fingertips spread out, facing the sun and breathing in the incredible aliveness of the sea, of the ocean, of the sun, of the wind." Her brother calls that gesture of their father's the "sky hug," which he practiced often.

Julia's father died in January 2021. His loss was a great devastation for Julia, made worse for the distance and the quarantine, which prohibited gathering for a service. "I would go on walks to try and soothe myself by immersing myself in nature and feel its energy." Julia noticed the immensity of her grief made it difficult to see color. "After he passed, I was unable to take any color photographs. I remember going on walks in the snow, and I could see beauty, I could recognize it, but I could only see it in black and white."

Without family around her to normalize and share in her grief, there were moments when she doubted whether she should give it the space it needed because it took her attention away from other people. She remembered thinking, "I know my sadness is inconvenient for some people around me. It was really hard for my boyfriend; he really was missing me and longing for that happy-go-lucky person that I was before. But I felt I am not going to rush through this. It is extremely important that I feel into this." It was important "because in the darkness and the loss and the grieving, I was finding the exquisiteness of my lived connection to life."

Several years before her father died, a friend wrote her a letter after she had lost her own father and said, "I really wish that people wouldn't rush their mourning process, that they take their time, because in the mourning process there is so much important information. You learn deeply about yourself, you learn deeply about life." What Julia learned during that time was about the legacy her father left her and her children. "My father truly believed in awe and the wonder of beauty and of nature. Finding that lesson helped pull me back into my life."

Performing the eulogy a year later in New York was an important part of Julia's healing process. "Reading the eulogy felt like a mature performance. When I first stepped up, I just took deep breaths to help myself first. Then I connected with everyone in the church. I looked around the room, and that seemed to help everyone settle in. There was a performative thing at the end where I invited people to do the sky hug. And after that, I really felt the deep processing of my father's loss become more concrete and materialized through the enactment of that speech and sharing it with so many people."

A year and a half later, Julia said she felt a renewed sense of vitality. Taking her camera into the park, she remembered how it appeared to her after her father died compared to what it looked like now. "The trees had been pruned back, and they looked like angry fists against the sky. And now, a year later, those same fists had sprouted hundreds of new leafy fingers. And it was so beautiful, it was just bursting with color. I could appreciate the color and feel the aliveness."

In the first months after her father's death, Julia's observations of beauty would open only to sadness. "At first, the raw experience of vulnerability would have me weeping at how beautiful the light was coming in the window in the morning. Maybe it was looking for traces of my father." But it transformed over time "into looking for traces of why life is worth living." She describes having this extreme relationship to beauty now, which she attributes to having given herself the time to be with "the extreme quality of the loss."

Reflecting on a morning practice she has created with her father's "sky hug," she said, "It's in my relationship to my father that I go out there and say, 'Okay, what does today have for me?' It's wonderful to feel the difference. It has become a beautiful embodiment of his legacy, but then also a practice for me also to feel life and feel where I'm in relationship to life."

The legacy of her father is also embodied in Julia's work. Beauty is still at the core of what she is creating because she believes in its power to ignite the kind of emotions that create connection between people. "Beauty can be very disarming. When I did work on the street in New York, beautiful performance installations helped to disarm people who might not have been open to a certain topic or certain history. Something beautiful helped them to feel more open."

What Julia makes now is coming from a desire to be in a more intimate relationship with herself and to make work from her personal experience. "I think what's made me an even better artist now is the question, what can I speak through my own body's experience, or my own soul's experience of this topic or this theme?" Now, Julia is using her artistry to make ceramic ceremonial vessels that help people experience beauty in connection to themselves, to each other, and to the sacred in all of life.

BRAVING CREATIVITY

Julia's story is a beautiful example of navigating from the heart. When she commits to her grieving process, she experiences a new depth of awareness about her connection to herself, to beauty, and to the world. This awareness of her belonging to something greater empowers her to trust her own soul's ability to connect with her purpose every day.

NAVIGATE

There is something so sacred about our time with grief after loss, because for many of us, it doesn't hang around forever in that constant heavy state. At some point, what Julia describes as the "extreme quality of loss" will lessen and fade. It will eventually become "concrete and materialized" through the many ways we will ritualize and remember our loss.

Julia shows us how, when we spend time in grief, we access something greater than the pain of the loss itself. Our heart has the capacity to feel an "extreme" connection to grief and to beauty, and to hold both even when it seems too much to bear. When we have the courage to inhabit the darkness of loss, we appreciate the magnitude and vibrancy of the beauty that is also always here.

The embodiment of the "sky hug" that Julia now practices helps her feel a connection to all of life and creates the capacity within her to experience all that arrives on any given day for her to hold.

EMPOWER

You can sense that Julia trusts where her heart is taking her because she registers the "exquisite" synergies in nature that enrich her experience of sorrow and of beauty. In the darkness of her grief, a clarity emerges when she experiences the beauty around her as a confirmation of her own worth and of the wondrous proof of a life worth living. That very self-worth empowers Julia to put her own body's knowledge at the center of her life and her work, which is to declare the value of intimate connection to herself and in her relationships and in relationship to the world around her.

HOW DO YOU BRAVE CREATIVITY?

What is the most extreme experience of beauty you have ever had? Did it come with an awareness of loss? Try looking out toward the world with arms outstretched in a "sky hug." What shifts when you do this?

CHIE FUEKI

*I am kind of idealistic, because what I am describing
doesn't really exist until I visually put it down
in the object of painting.
I think painting is a form that is capable of describing
a kind of space that might not be exactly easy to locate.*

—CHIE FUEKI, PAINTER

Painter Chie Fueki experienced the most profound change in her life before she started kindergarten. In 1976, Chie's father moved the family from their home in Japan to São Paulo, Brazil, where the company he worked for had invested and where many other Japanese businessmen lived with their families for brief periods in South America. The expectation was that her family would only stay in Brazil for a few years. Chie said, "I was always prepared to go back to Japan at any moment." Years turned into decades. Chie watched her childhood friends come and go after only brief stays, but "I ended up not ever going back permanently."

Chie received her BFA from The Ringling College of Art and Design and an MFA from Yale University. She is the inaugural recipient of the 2021 Joan Mitchell Fellowship and the John Simon Guggenheim Memorial Foundation Fellowship, and a two-time Purchase Prize recipient from the American Academy of Art and Letters. Chie has also received a Rosenthal Family Foundation Award from the

American Academy of Arts and Letters. Her work is included in permanent collections of the Modern Art Museum of Fort Worth, TX; Orlando Museum of Art, FL; San Jose Museum of Art, CA; the Hirshhorn Museum, DC; and the Pizzuti Collection at Columbus Museum of Art, OH. Chie also has public artwork at PS 92Q, Queens, NY, and at the HHS Lerner Children Pavilion in New York City.

Born in Yokohama, Japan, Chie grew up in an expat Japanese community in São Paulo, Brazil. During elementary school, Chie said, "I was secretly depressed. I remember looking out at the moon at night, over the lights of the city, and wondering about my feelings." She credits a shift in her outlook to a visit to the São Paulo Museum of Art, where her parents often took her and her sister. "I remember feeling like I didn't really know where I belonged. Then I saw some of the paintings in the museum, especially those by Van Gogh, and I understood that space. I didn't really know what that meant, but looking at those paintings, I felt okay. Van Gogh made me see that there may be a space somewhere in this world that would make sense to me. I didn't think I would become a painter in order make the kind of place I wanted to be."

When she was a young student, Chie didn't think she would be an artist at all. In her home, there was an emphasis on education. "I was a good student, and I think my parents were hoping that my sister and I would go to a Japanese university." At the American International High School in São Paulo, Chie took an art class. "I had some space in my credits senior year in high school. Who would have known that an art class would ignite something in me?" One of

Chie's first assignments "was to draw my left hand with my right hand from observation with a graphite pencil. I made a pretty terrible drawing of my own hand, but something shifted in my head that was significant. At that moment, I knew this is the direction I want to pursue." She laughed and said, "Even though I didn't know how to draw yet."

Now that Chie understands art history, she can see that her interest in Van Gogh and many other post-impressionists' work might have been an attraction to the kind of intersection that brought many impressionists to Japanese Ukiyo-e. "I am interested in the visual dialogue and intersection between several different sources or cultures. Until recently, I didn't consciously think that what I am describing in my paintings is that kind of in-between space where a shift happens."

Because she grew up in a very close Japanese community in Brazil, Chie said, "I'm not even sure what makes me Japanese." Her sense of belonging was so challenged as a little girl that she wonders if "that cemented in me a sort of liminality, of being in-between worlds."

Since Chie was born, her grandmother had been a very present and important maternal figure. Her grandmother died when she was six, just shortly after the family moved to Brazil. The cremation ceremony ritual made an imprint on Chie. "The cremation process allows for some of the bones to remain." She recalled how the mourners and closest family collected the remains. "We used chopsticks to pick pieces from the remaining bones and place them in a vessel to bring to the family burial ground."

Chie said the Buddhist name her grandmother was given for the afterlife translates to "Compassionate Light of the Moon." As a child, "every time the moon rose over São Paulo, I was connecting to my grandmother from my bedroom window, and I was connecting to Japan from São Paulo." Of the image of the moon, she said, "It was a way for me to connect to some space that was in-between, but it also created a bridge to a place that I could visit mentally." Over the years, "it was kind of unconsciously chosen, but I have made a lot of paintings of the moon."

Chie's current work is a series she made from her home in Beacon, New York, which was created during the early COVID-pandemic lockdown. Inspired from a home installation in the living room of her apartment overlooking Beacon Mountain, *Mountain Altar* (2020) depicts the large picture window in her apartment. The upper corners of the frame are adorned with large black ribbons—94x64 inches—of mulberry paper, which are painted with silver acrylic stripes, dashes and hearts, and ornamental flowers. The windowpane is adorned with a few dozen small black hearts and sections of painted lattice. In the frame, the windowsill and underneath a bench holds potted plants and other ephemera, including a card propped up showing with a front-facing image depicting three eyes looking into the room. A coffee table with a glass surface sits in the foreground and reflects the picture window and the mountain outside. At night, the moon rises over the mountain and completes the *Mountain Alter*.

The collection currently in place in her Beacon studio is a series of artworks made from meticulously layered papers, paints, and color pencil. Delicate pin drops of paint create starbursts and pop imagery throughout the artworks. "My dad thinks I've painted Mount Fuji." Each piece, like the *Mountain Altar*, is framed by a windowsill and includes abstracts and still lifes of her potted plants. The moon shows up in most of the paintings, sometimes in several locations and in different sizes. The appearance of the moon in her work surprises even Chie. "Oh, I didn't even realize I painted this moon. Look there is one!"

The mountains painted in this collection have eyes that gaze at the viewer, which are also the reflection of the viewer's own eyes in the window. In some cases, "they are calling the viewer toward the mountain, and in others, the mountain is gazing into the domestic space." The mountain is a meaningful central focus for Chie. "It became so important during lockdown, nature and its significance, along with the moon, which is so much more vast than we are."

A concept in Japanese arts and culture is the idea of "Mono No Aware," which translates to "the pathos of things." Chie said, "I didn't think that was why I became a painter, to process my sadness and those feelings of longing for a place that felt like home when I was a child, but I can tell now, after working for twenty-five years, that those early experiences inform a kind of space that I am trying to describe through the act of painting."

Reflecting on her identification with impermanence and her desire for belonging, she said, "Just by looking at Van Gogh's portraits or a landscape painting at São Paulo Museum of Art, I sensed a kind of place that didn't really exist before he painted it but that I belonged to." What she has come to realize is "I'm actually always hoping to make a place, make a space for somebody that needs the kind of space I did."

Behind Chie in her studio, she showed me *Pink Moon*, 2022. Chie approaches her painting process now from a feeling place from which "I know exactly what I need to do one step at time. It's only a little step forward. I don't know what it's going to look like as a whole at the end, but just by following and trusting, I know that it will come together." As she paints, she is also aware of thoughts that urge her to use caution. "There is another side of my brain that yells at me. I feel irresponsible painting that way. But I know that is the only way I can find the kind of painting I'm truly interested in."

That is the process by which Chie surrenders to the painting and allows it to direct the process. "It's different than flow; this is more about choosing to let the painting take over. Sometimes, she said, "I'm sitting through a process just feeling completely anxious." But if she allows the process to unfold, she finds the place she is looking for. "If I don't interfere with myself, all the parts almost miraculously fall into place, and they come together."

"It's a mindset" is how Chie explains her process now, which integrates the liminality she identifies with the transience she often feels in her own life. "Of course, I need to physically work on the painting, but I don't control the work. The painting itself is telling me what to do, and the unconscious part of my brain is telling me what to do." That end result is born in-between the past and some place she can't name but to which she belongs. The paintings always land somewhere, but, Chie said, "I don't know how to locate that place even today."

BRAVING CREATIVITY

Chie realizes, in retrospect, her paintings reflect a kind of unconscious longing to create a space where her heart feels it belongs. Navigation and play are the primary pillars she works with to enter a transient mindset that allows what she creates to unfold in that in-between place that feels like home.

NAVIGATE

Chie's young heart points her toward her bedroom window to take solace in the moon where she can be with her grandmother and back home in Japan. The longing in her heart for permanence, acceptance, and belonging moves with her as she searches for that place in her heart. It is in a painting by Van Gogh at the São Paulo Museum that Chie has a poignant resonant experience of recognition that clarifies her longing to belong to a place like the one that it exists in his paintings. This subtle and persistent longing in her heart is the compass Chie follows in her life and work to create such a space for someone else who longs for "the same space" that Chie does.

PLAY

Chie describes herself as an idealist because she paints to create a place she can only ever know in her heart. Her strategy, then, is to do exactly as all the artists in these stories do in transition, which is to start with a blank slate and plan for no "thing" to result. The intention to stand in that in-between space opens the reservoir of her unconscious creativity and creates synergy between her and the painting itself. Chie demonstrates the fortitude to endure the anxiety that erupts during her process because she believes a shift will occur that will satisfy her longing.

HOW DO YOU BRAVE CREATIVITY?

What feelings do you experience as you sit through your creative process? What does that tell you about your own curiosity or fortitude? Is there something intangible that you long to create?

L M FELDMAN

But suddenly today, there it was: the itch
of curiosity and self-expression.
So I sat down and wrote three pages.
A small triumph in the direction of restored capacity.
—L M FELDMAN, PLAYWRIGHT

In March 2020, the week the COVID pandemic sent everyone indoors, playwright and circus artist L M Feldman suffered a blow when her ten-year relationship to her life and artistic partner suddenly unraveled. That was the week, "everything ground to a halt. My entire life sort of exploded."

L M is a queer, feminist playwright, dramaturg, and circus artist living in Philadelphia. She has been nominated for the Herb Alpert Award, Wendy Wasserstein Prize, Venturous fellowship, Susan Smith Blackburn Prize, Barrie and Bernice Stavis Playwriting Award, the New York Innovative Theatre Award, and the Doris Wilson Independent Playwright Award. L M is a graduate of Cornell University, the Yale School of Drama MFA program, and the New England Center for Circus Arts.

Nobody who knows L M now would say she is shy, but growing up in Miami, Florida, she didn't take many big embodied risks. "I remember thinking that as soon as I go to college, I will say 'Yes!' to theater." Choosing to attend a college in snowy western New York was the most fitting location for L M because "I was a plaid flannel, corduroy-wearing, tea-and-cider-sipping dyke, so I went as far north of Miami as possible." An English Studies major at Cornell, she started taking acting classes. She remembers her acting teacher saying, "You're a playwright, not an actor," which at the time, she said, "I was not super excited to hear."

L M didn't take her acting teacher's feedback to heart right away. She explored other ways to apply her love of words and writing. She took several genre-specific classes in her major. She realized, "that I'm not really super great at these genres. I'm not shining at them." L M considered theater more broadly. First, she admitted, "I'm replaceable as an actor." In a final effort to find a place in the theater that would have her exclaim "Yes!" she tried a playwriting course and, she recalled, "I was like, 'Oh my God. Yes!' It combines everything I love with everything I love!'"

At the tail end of her tenure at the Yale School of Drama where she received her MFA in Playwriting, she met the Tony-award-winning queer feminist playwright and performance artist Lisa Kron who recommended she go see a show by the feminist Brooklyn-based acrobatic dance company, LAVA. "I didn't know something like LAVA existed, and it rocked my world." She promised herself that if she ever moved to New York, she would find a way to train with LAVA.

Several years later, in 2010, L M was in New York teaching playwriting as an adjunct at Bard College and was accepted into a work-study program to train with LAVA for a summer. That is where she met her romantic partner, who was already a trained trapeze soloist. L M completed full-time training at the New England Center for Circus Arts. After that, she and her partner formed a duo. They performed together at the Chicago Contemporary Circus Festival, the Golden Karl International Circus Festival in Riga, Latvia, and the Daidogei World Cup in Japan. Over the next ten years, she said, "We really intertwined our lives and our careers and our home and our families."

The depression that arrived with the breakup was familiar. "I had felt depression before, so I knew the terrain, even though this was much more life shattering than anything I had experienced before." She was self-aware enough to create a supportive framework for the road she sensed would be ahead. "I know what I'm like in a storm and so I prepared in case it happened. And then it happened."

L M and her partner lived on the top floor of a three-story home that looked like "the upside-down hull of a ship." The couple that owned the house and their teenage daughter had become family. She let them know what would feel supportive, and they jumped in with some practical advice. "The first thing we will do is repaint the walls. Then we'll move the furniture around." They helped L M create a healing space, lent her their guest bedroom, and shared meals together. When she was ready, L M tried to transition back to her bedroom from her housemate's guest room on the second floor. "At first, I could only sit on the bed with a book or on a phone call. I did that for a few weeks. Then I was ready to try to lie down on it."

L M and her partner decided to let their friends know of their split together. They had nurtured a close community of friends and colleagues through their artistic work. They loved hosting "soup swaps," where invited guests brought their six quarts of soup and then picked straws to see who'd get which of their friends' favorite soups. "We'd swap and nosh, kibitz and drink." Swaps were paired with game night or story prompts that invited sharing. "It was a way of bringing community and nourishment together. Amazing women, queer folks, gender non-conformers from every decade of life."

These gatherings and their community dispersed at the outset of the pandemic, as did the creative community and all the potential work and productions L M had created through her playwriting residencies, circus, and teaching gigs. It was hard for her to accept this forced containment. At that time, too, she was recovering from a recent shoulder injury. "I couldn't even hang from a bar." She identified strongly with the physical and academic rigor she excelled at and missed the energy of moving multiple projects along in the dynamic creative environments in which she thrived. The one thing she could do in stillness from the desk in her room was also the one thing she couldn't touch. She told her agent, "I don't think I can write anything. I don't think I can meet this deadline. I don't think I can. I can't even hold things without dropping them."

L M's agent helped her get the project extensions she needed, but she felt she needed to do *something* with this time that would help her process her loss. She recalled a friend once saying, "A person doesn't have to know how to heal in order to heal." She leaned on the faith that other people had in her ability to recover from this loss, or, she said, "Maybe

I relied on faith that humans heal." Either way, adopting a mindset of "not knowing" really helped her just be where she was in her process.

That's when L M decided to photograph her day-to-day grief and healing experiences in movement. She posted sparse images and reflections in a private Instagram account that functioned as a visual journal. "I knew I needed to make art as a way of expressing this transition. This seemed like a morsel way of doing it. The morsel way of being physical and embodied."

L M proposed to write a ninety-day photo-journal with captions. To her, it was just enough of a literary expression that she could contemplate completing one entry every day. The initial ninety-day duration was decided based on a time in the past when she underwent a period of rehabilitation from a major injury and surgery. She remembered it took about ninety days before she felt she had "turned the corner in terms of my mental outlook about my recovery." So that was the length of time she set for the journal.

Day one of the journal was titled "When Things Fall Apart. And So Do You," which was accompanied by a picture of L M suspending herself in a plank position with her torso and legs arching upward toward the ceiling like the bow of an arrow. It was important to L M that the images did most of the work. "I wanted an image each day. And I wanted it to be something with my body as a way to hold onto movement as expression."

The Instagram journal was just enough of a creative expression that it felt good, but not so much that it felt impossible to approach. "If I could put it into writing, it felt a little bit like a literary expression." The journal was completed on day one hundred ninety-four and was installed on Instagram over six months. Just shy of seven months, L M posted an entry to celebrate completing her first pull-up since her injury. Then the day came when, she wrote, "Today—for the first time since losing my life partner, my trust, my productions and my career, and home and identity as I knew it—I felt a tiny pang of hunger to write dialogue. I haven't wanted to write a play in nine months."

She described the process of transition from the first entry through to the last as a revelation. She marveled, "If I take grief and pain and I turn it into art, then it alchemizes into something positive?" In response to her visual journal, people with totally different circumstances began to share their stories. "People talked about the kinds of losses that don't often get talked about publicly or that we don't want to talk about much. And it was really helpful."

L M describes this part of her transformation as "terra nova." Now forty-three, she feels like she did in her early thirties when she was an emerging artist who didn't know the basics of writing a grant application or a website, or even a bio and an artist statement. "I've been here before. Well, not exactly here, but I've been somewhere like here." For someone as directed as L M, being at this juncture is unsettling. "I don't usually find myself in a place where I don't know at all what I want. And I'm in that place right now."

Her strategy has always been to ask the big questions. The one that strikes her as the most essential right now is "Do I take all of my circus life and give it a beautiful funeral and then direct all of my energy into theater and performance instead?" That's not something she has an answer to yet.

She can, however, offer a tentative "yes" to something new—writing a two-person play. "My agent has been nudging me for years to do it. I'm pretty committed to making that happen this year, somehow."

BRAVING CREATIVITY

Part of the liberating power of change for L M is the opportunity to discover who she really is once her identity was shattered by the end of her partnership and because of a worldwide pandemic. She embarked on a process of transition that relied on play and navigation to take her in morsels toward some place new.

LIBERATE

When the shock of a loss catapults L M into a crisis of identity, she is challenged to undo all she thought was certain and face all she doesn't know for sure anymore. In this story, L M describes how challenging it was to compute a stark new reality that appeared before her in what seemed like an instant: No relationship. No work. No community.

"Who am I now?" is the question that weighs on her greatly. "Who am I now without my partner and the life we intertwined and enjoyed together? Who am I now without commitments and a plan? Who am I now without the ability to do a pull-up or to write?" Behind these questions is the answer that unfolds gently over a period of almost a year as L M brings her awareness and self-compassion to the emergence of a new identity and a new beginning.

PLAY

L M embarks upon a ritualized reflection. The Instagram journal entries and images alchemize over time to create a healing balm when her other avenues for self-soothing are not accessible to her in this in-between time. After many small reflections and morsels of movement, a bit of light comes through—a friendly note of gratitude, an idea for a piece of dialogue. L M had never used Instagram in this way. There was nothing she could point to and say, "That! That worked, so I'll do that again." It was just the one small thing she *could* do, and she did it one hundred ninety-four times in a row, and that was how she caught her breath and let some light in.

NAVIGATE

L M trusted the intuition that told her to make art from this transition. Without access to the grand embodied movement of her physical expression or ability to write elevated literary prose, she decided on a "morsel" approach. She trusted her heart, the Universe, and other people's wisdom that she would heal without having to know how. With that surrender, she gave over to the one hundred ninety-four days of reflection and then an invitation arrived—to write a play. And not just any play—a two-person play.

HOW DO YOU BRAVE CREATIVITY?

When have you felt lost? Has there been a time when one small ritual or a set of steps taken in morsels let some light in? What piece of inner wisdom or outer guidance have you marveled at receiving?

DESIRE

There comes a time in [a woman's life]
[when she] feels restricted, restrained by self and/or others,
yet at the same time, she feels she is made for something more;
that this can't be "all there is,"
that instead her birthright is trying to come to the surface.
—DR. CLARISSA PINKOLA ESTÉS

Early in my forties, my therapist gave me more than a vocabulary lesson. She posed a simple question: "Do you feel entitled to have your needs met?" She might as well have been speaking to me from under water. I didn't understand the question. Entitlement presupposes that we have a right to our own experience and that our own experience has worth because it belongs to us. How was I not aware of something as central to my experience as my needs? Not having the courage to voice my needs in relationships didn't mean I didn't have them—but that I feared them. In order to mitigate that threat, I found workarounds. And workarounds, when it comes to needs of the heart, only create more confusion and disconnection.

The question my therapist asked created a small fracture in the layers of beliefs and patterns that kept my voice in the dark. Meditation teacher and author of *Trusting the Gold* Tara Brach tells a story about a large statue of Buddha in Bangkok, Thailand, which for centuries appeared to be made of clay. When the statue "began to crack due to heat and drought" in the 1950s, a "gleam of gold" was revealed. Under threat of an impending invasion, monks in a nearby monastery applied plaster and clay to hide the beauty and value of what was a huge solid gold statue (Brach 2022, 2). With each deepening crack in my own layers of protection, I began turning toward the light of my gleaming desire shining through.

When our identity breaks down after big change, we have a chance to get into an honest relationship with ourselves and decide who we desire to become in transition. In her identity as a queer Black woman, author and founder of the Center for Transformation Change, Reverend Angel Kyodo Williams said, "I didn't have the entitlement to take some things for granted. What became clear to me is that I had to ask all of the questions." The central question comes down to this: "Do you know who you really are? And do you want to know?" (Williams 2021, 56.33).

Are we willing to see things as they really are—the good, the bad, and the ugly—all of it? Behind all my fear and striving, behind my self-doubt and control, who am I? Did I, in the identity I was attached to before the crisis, collude, coerce, or collaborate in the circumstances that contributed to the suffering my husband and I experienced? Does my fear of knowing and expressing my needs in relationships continue even now to reduce me to tactics that occlude my courageous and authentic expression, my desire for connection?

Our desire to live beyond all or part of the identity we ascribed or belonged to *is its own catalyst*. You don't need a crisis to rock your foundation in order to challenge your beliefs, but something has to happen to ignite the fire within you to claim your desire as worthy of exploration and expression.

Writer and author Elizabeth Gilbert, in her book *Magic Lessons*, uses the term *creative entitlement* to describe the experience of "believing that you are allowed to be here, and that—merely by being here—you are allowed to have a voice and a vision of your own" (Gilbert 2015, 92). As you plumb your worth up from the dark into the radiant light, can you sense that you are becoming more of who you really are?

In the stories that follow, see if you can identify the catalyst that causes the artist to break with part or all of her identity in order to give voice to who she is becoming. The artists in this section are on a path to giving courageous voice to a vision of their own. Yanira Castro breaks from the dance field to create a new way to make work that honors her desire to create spaces for civic dialogue through performance engagement with audiences; Playwright Dipika Guha confronts her own and her parents' fears that becoming a writer will lead to destitution and claims her voice as a playwright; Sculptor Ada Pilar Cruz commits to making her mark in clay by defending her choice to create work that expresses the language in her heart.

DIPIKA GUHA

It is an enormous gamble to stretch into
a future that you can't see.
And at the same time, the stretching validates
a deep commitment to who you've always been.
In a strange way, the past and the future
come together in that moment of instability.
If you let it, and if you're ready,
it can crystallize, and magic happens.

—DIPIKA GUHA, PLAYWRIGHT

At twenty-two years of age, Dipika was living in London and working for the British Broadcasting Corporation (BBC). Her parents thought it was a dream job. But Dipika said, "It was absolutely soul-destroying. I was in a moment of enormous suffering, and I kind of didn't know why." An actor from the repertory company, a woman whom Dipika had only met a few times in passing before, knocked on the glass partition of her office cubicle and said, "I have something for you." The woman left a copy of Julia Cameron's *The Artist's Way* on Dipika's desk. Within a year of working with that book, Dipika said, "I had a scholarship to Harvard where I wrote my first play; it changed the direction of my life."

Dipika Guha is a Los Angeles-based, Calcutta-born playwright raised in Russia, India, and the United Kingdom.

She earned her undergraduate degree at University College, London, won a Frank Knox Fellowship to Harvard University, received the Adele Kellenberg Fellowship in Playwriting from Brown University, as well as her MFA from the Yale School of Drama under Paula Vogel. She has been awarded numerous fellowships and residencies, including a current Venturous Fellow with the Lark Play Development Center, as a Hodder Fellow at the Lewis Center for the Arts at Princeton University, and as the inaugural Shakespeare's Sister Playwriting Fellow. Dipika has received recent commissions from Berkeley Rep, Playwrights Horizons, South Coast Rep, Manhattan Theatre Club, and Barrington Stage, among others. Her selected television credits include having written for *American Gods*, *Sneaky Pete*, *Black Monday*, and *The Marvelous Mrs. Maisel*, and projects in development at FilmNation and A24.

From around the age of five, Dipika recalled creating plays in her living room. "Whenever my parents had people around, I'd bombard them with little shows I had written." Reflecting on that time, Dipika believes her interest in storytelling was always evident, but "I just was too scared to see it and say it and acknowledge what that meant." Becoming an artist seemed to be an impossible proposition. Nobody Dipika knew pursued a career that didn't guarantee financial stability. "There was absolutely no road to follow."

Dipika's parents considered her job at the BBC to be "the pinnacle for me." Her grandparents and great-grandparents were refugees when India was partitioned in 1947. They grew up in a generation that faced the financial devastation and brutality of the British occupation but never talked about it.

She believes her parents' anxiety about her job security had its roots in their experience. "In the massive Indian middle class, the pressure to accumulate has been very deep, which has manifested I think as 'do the conventional thing.' Because one generation ago, nobody had anything; people were starving."

Dipika also felt she inherited the pain of the "massively misogynist culture" of her parents' and grandparents' upbringing. "I'm the first person in my familial history to have a choice of spouse." By the time she got to the BBC, "All of the silencing had accumulated in me. I was in a moment of enormous suffering. I was twenty-two. I kind of didn't know why I felt all of it."

She reached a tipping point at the BBC. "I felt the immediate and absolute soul-destroying impact of British patriarchy and racism." While she was there, she realized, "Oh, I am never going to be able to speak in my own voice in Britain." She was grieving for what seemed to be her fate under those circumstances. "I was feeling that I hadn't said anything, I hadn't written anything, and I had no sense that I could."

Then *The Artist's Way* came to her desk. "Someone who I had met only briefly (Coleen Prendergast, who was to become a close friend in the years that followed) looked at me and said, 'Oh, she's in trouble.'" They'd met only once in passing and spoke nothing of Dipika's secret desire to become a playwright. Dipika credits *The Artist's Way* with changing the trajectory of her life. "It was like someone shattered the window open."

At that time, though, her parents didn't know Dipika was struggling emotionally. "I felt so uncomfortable at the BBC.

It felt like my whole body was on fire." In her silence, she set herself the task of writing "morning pages," a core practice of *The Artist's Way*. "I did it with such a desperation. I followed it religiously. That is how I taught myself how to write. I wrote in a stream of consciousness for ten minutes a day. And it changed everything." Dipika described what happened next as being almost magical. "I know it sounds insane, but by committing to morning pages, it was like I touched a current of truth buried inside myself."

Dipika attributes the many synchronicities and coincidences during that time to her work in *The Artist's Way*. During the period when she was writing her morning pages, she accompanied her boss at the BBC to The Royal Court Theater in London to take meeting notes. At the meeting, the theater director mentioned the Royal Court's Young Writer's Program. That caught Dipika's attention. "I looked up and I said, 'I'd really like to do that.'"

She almost didn't recognize herself in that moment. "It was like something went off in my head that said clearly, 'I want to do it,' which I don't think I would ever have done at a meeting with my boss before those months writing daily. It felt like an insane request." She hadn't written a play yet, and one was required to apply, but the program director, Ola Animashaun, turned to Dipika and said, "Okay, I'll send you an invitation."

No one ever asked Dipika for a play when she arrived at The Royal Court. She was excited to study, but right from the start, she hit a roadblock. "A teacher told me that I had 'a resistance to story.' He believed that there was only one 'right' way to write a play. And at that time, I felt like I couldn't do it. It was a very discouraging experience. So, I arrived not having written anything. And I left not having written anything, because I was just so intimidated."

"It was all *The Artist's Way*," Dipika said of the courage that continued to propel her forward, even after her time at The Royal Court. She applied to a dramaturgy program in the United States. "At that point, I had no real idea what dramaturgy was. I just thought it meant apprenticing in theater. And I thought, *Well, if I can't write, maybe I can be an apprentice.*"

She was accepted into the dramaturgy program at Harvard, but they had no funding to support her during her studies. "I had to decline because I couldn't afford it." The head of the program invited Dipika for coffee when he was visiting London. He encouraged her to apply for scholarships to support her studies. "I left that meeting with two feelings, that probably dramaturgy wasn't for me and that I was absolutely going to apply to the program."

"I don't understand these things," Dipika said of the kind of desire and intuition that kept her going even when so much was unknown. She was shortlisted for three fellowships but didn't get any of them. Dipika attributed that outcome to a limiting belief. "Someone told me I couldn't write, and on some level, I believed that." Dipika heard that part of her say, *It's no wonder that everybody's ambivalent about you. Because you don't know. You don't even know yourself that you can do it.* For a week, "I wept and meditated. Then a shift occurred in my heart when I saw what I believed about myself. I believed I couldn't write. Acknowledging that belief shifted something. Then the phone rang, and it was the scholarship committee. They said, 'Someone's dropped out.'"

It turned out that the dramaturgy program she applied for was no longer available, but she was invited to use the year-long fellowship however she wanted. "The dean of the school, Margaret Gill, said to me, 'I'm not going to ask you what you did with this time. Just come see me at the end of the year.'" It was another gift. "I didn't have to do the thing that I didn't want to do. And I was able to use that time to write a play. I scrambled to put a little curriculum together for myself, and I wrote."

When confronted with course options at Harvard, her old doubts threatened to sabotage this opportunity. She thought, *If I choose these courses while I'm here, I could prepare myself to go to law school. If I put these ducks in a row, maybe something more sensible would arise.* Despite feeling unprepared to make sense of the opportunities now available to her, she felt clear about one thing. "I was in the driver's seat. I will say what happens this year." Being so far from home provided a healthy distance from her parents' concerns and her own personal fear of judgment. "If I failed, no one would have to know. It would all be over in nine months either way. And that really, really, really freed me up."

"I think of Harvard now as a hatchery," Dipika said of that year. "That dark place that art needs to grow. That place where you don't talk about your desires. Sometimes in talking about them, it loses the potency of their directionality. Because your desire is a direction. It's a directive."

With an expanse of time and the permission to explore, Dipika gathered her confidence. She chose classes in theater history, vocal production, and post-colonial literature. As she studied, "an inner honing happened." She worked quietly toward finding the idea for the play she would write. "But before that, I had to get into a playwriting class."

She hadn't written a play yet, and she still didn't really understand what was blocking her from doing the thing she was driving so concertedly toward. When Dipika came to London, she was seventeen. "I didn't know enough to parse out what was happening in terms of class and privilege and money." Early in school, she learned how "text was king in Britain. There was no room for interpretation. We began with Anglo Saxon and ended with Toni Morrison. It's a straight line." It wasn't until much later that those lessons were challenged when she realized "there are lenses we can read from. There is a feminist lens, you can have a Marxist lens on something or a post-colonial lens." It wasn't until her first playwriting class at Harvard that Dipika was able to integrate that message into her own writing voice.

Dipika was surprised when she saw her playwriting teacher at her first class. "In England, you don't become a full professor until you are in your fifties or sixties. I was so devastated when this young preppy guy walked in. I was like, 'He's too young to know anything!'" She describes how Professor Sam Marks' approach shattered Dipika's writer's block wide open at their first meeting. "I had started to say something about myself, and he said, 'It doesn't matter. I don't need to know your biography. Biography has nothing to do with what you write.'"

She realized in that moment that she believed she had to write the way the patriarchy saw her and how other people viewed her. She thought her writing had to reflect what she looked like. "I felt whatever I wrote had to be a one-to-one with what I looked like. And what I look like was not my life experience. I had grown up in a bunch of places, and it wasn't going to match the British Indian experience that people might think that I would have." Dipika was euphoric. "That one sentence, it was so liberating. I didn't have to write about my own experience. I could just make something. I could breathe. It was so freeing."

Now liberated from the belief she had to write a certain way, Dipika could explore her imagination and who she wanted to become now that she was not locked into one way of being or being seen. "I just sat in that little dorm room and wrote. What is better than that? God, there's nothing better than being able to own an hour."

Dipika kept much of her journey private from her parents. "I didn't really talk about what I was going to do or how I was doing it, because I didn't know. And I was *deeply* afraid, deeply, deeply afraid. And I knew that their fear would ignite mine." But it was also because Dipika hadn't accumulated any evidence of her talent yet. "I didn't have the magic external validation or the big show I could point to and say, 'Oh, everyone else thinks that I should keep doing this.'"

As difficult as they found the not knowing, Dipika said, "My mum says she's no longer afraid. I think, at some point, for both of them, they stopped being afraid, and maybe that's been the victory."

She credits the power of her commitment to herself for enduring the challenges in her work and life over these past few decades.

"My decision to commit to this path influenced the shape of my life. It was not going to be about whether I could afford to do it or not, or whether I had time. It wasn't going to be about any of that. I was going to do it, no matter what. That was the road that gave me everything I needed. That commitment."

BRAVING CREATIVITY

Dipika's heart takes her on a journey to find her voice. *The Artist's Way* provides a lifeline that engages her hunger for liberation from the oppressive societal and cultural norms of the British patriarchy and the inherited trauma she carried as a result. Dipika becomes willing to take bigger and bigger risks to strengthen her commitment to her desire to become a writer.

LIBERATE

Dipika's nervous system was under threat. Her emerging identity terrorized into silence. In those months before *The Artist's Way* came to her desk, she felt the *suppression* of her voice and also the *threat* her voice presented to her parents' sense of security and to the patriarchy she grew up within. Over time, Dipika confronted not only her own fear, but also her parents' fear and a constellation of inherited fears that came before them in order to find the courage to commit to her path. The risk she is willing to take is her parents' disapproval and her own failure.

When she recognizes her self-abandonment during the fellowship application process to Harvard, she mourns the belief she carries that she can't be a writer. "I felt a sadness that I believed that about myself." By giving herself space to grieve, she connects to the courage to follow her heart one step further again.

Later, Dipika notices the limiting thoughts that attempt to undermine her course selection at Harvard. What is important to note in both examples is there is also a part of her that is a witness to those thoughts. The part of her that is the witness is not afraid. That part, she says, "Is in the driver's seat."

NAVIGATE AND PLAY

Even before *The Artist's Way* arrives at Dipika's desk, she senses she is on the move. Writing her morning pages, she finds herself taking surprising intuitive risks. She has the exhilarating experience of asserting her presence, even when it seemed "insane" to make certain requests. Dipika's journey from the BBC to Professor Marks' class is full of ambiguity and synchronicities, discouragement and truth, and a growing courage to continue to try.

Professor Marks sets Dipika free from the constraints that held her voice in abeyance. Her journey shows us how to ignite desire in transition after the crisis of depression threatens to extinguish all hope of transformation. With *The Artist's Way* in hand, Dipika enters the darkness for wisdom until she emerges on her path, exactly in the right place and at the right time, to begin to write her first play.

HOW DO YOU BRAVE CREATIVITY?

What level of discomfort or silence have you tolerated for fear of upsetting other people? Do you have a compelling commitment? Is there something you learned from a professor that turned your perspective on its head?

YANIRA CASTRO

I feel like transformation is always happening.
I don't know that there's ever a moment where I have felt stable,
or have been like, 'Yes, this is it.' This is my path.
This is where I'm going.
Sometimes that movement has more of a peaceful feeling to it
than other times,
But it isn't ever still.

—YANIRA CASTRO, INTERDISCIPLINARY ARTIST

In 2005, choreographer Yanira Castro reached an inflection point in her career. She had just premiered a new dance piece, *Beacon*, at one of the then-preeminent New York City dance institutions for dance artists. "I just had my work presented by the organization I had long sought to present my work, and it had gone beautifully. But I was in debt, and I didn't make a cent. I was asking myself, 'How do I maintain this?'"

Yanira Castro is a Puerto Rican interdisciplinary artist making movement-based performance and work that begins in collaborative dialogue with other artmakers. She started making dance performances in the late 1990s and became a choreographer recognized in her field with prestigious funding awards and commissions, including the highly competitive 2022 Herb Alpert Award in Dance. Over her twenty-five-year career, she has created fifteen major performance works, which have been presented nationally and internationally. Yanira has been awarded creative residencies and fellowships, and she is a respected teacher and thought leader in her field.

Over a period of years, Yanira stepped outside of the format that had brought her professional recognition as a choreographer. At the time of her New York premiere of *Beacon* in 2005, Yanira was running her dance company, holding down another full-time job to generate income, and juggling any way she could to make up for the gaps in labor, attention, and funding that would make a long-term career as an artist viable. "I was rehearsing on the weekends and at night and writing grants at midnight to fund my dance company. I knew it wasn't sustainable. Something needed to change."

Yanira wasn't the only artist in her company burning the candle at both ends. The dancers who performed and cocreated works like *Beacon* were likewise juggling many competing demands to make ends meet, working jobs ranging from restaurant work to nannying, staying in shape for performing by attending classes, and addressing physical care needs akin to elite athletes with nothing like the training teams attached to sports franchises. For Yanira, what became particularly unconscionable was the fact that no matter how hard she worked—or how many commissions or grants or awards she won—it was unlikely to be enough to equitably compensate the labor involved in creating the work.

In a field where even giants are largely unrecognized by the general public, and the so-called "company model" with salaried performers is a fantasy barely dreamed of, Yanira increasingly came to terms with the reality that, despite her critical success and respect, she would never have the resources to act in alignment with what she knew was right. She would never be able to provide job security for the dance artists on whom her work depended.

The overwhelming expense of working in the traditional choreographic framework was just not financially tenable. "The traditional dance model depended on consistently winning grants, which is fine when you are the hot thing, but that kind of award comes once in a half-dozen years." Banking on future funding becomes even more challenging when your work is of an experimental nature, which Yanira said "made commercial success an unlikely road for me." In all cases, if you are to continue your work—in order to further develop it and continue to be competitive for grants—the expectation is for most of the artists involved to work on a near-voluntary basis.

More disturbing still was the message it communicated and the harm it perpetuated. Without a field-wide commitment to equitable dance practice and care of dance artists, the traditional company model fantasy was "not for me. It was not the path toward ethical, collaborative working relationships or toward experimentation and creativity."

Even so, it wasn't until 2008, when she became pregnant and her "day job" employer rejected her request to go part-time, that Yanira realized how much responsibility she had assumed. She realized "how silly it was to think I was going to be able to keep this full-time job and raise this child and continue to make dances in the way I had been making them." The reality of the unpaid labor she'd been absorbing—and asking others to absorb in kind—became starkly visible. After that, she said, "My work really did change drastically."

She knew what she was changing *from,* but she didn't know where she was headed because there was no map to follow. To forge a new path for artistic work not built on current practice is to swim against the current—particularly for someone who has achieved some level of success. "I had an instinct, but it's not like one day I set the intention to sit down and figure out the right way to do this. No, I muddled through a lot of it."

Those experiments led to the formation of *a canary torsi,* an informal group of collaborators gathered to engage with equal autonomy in a creative process. Yanira experimented with new ways of working. She consciously shifted away from a process that required months of working in a studio with a cast of dancers birthing a dance slowly through an evolution of shared physical language. Yanira first tried gathering dancers for rehearsal only during a time-bound residency period so the creative process would be contained within a shorter period more possible to appropriately compensate.

This is when Yanira broke with formal, audience-as-spectator style of dance performance and embraced a more nebulous lineage of artists who seek to experience performance "as a process for negotiation and transformation." No longer would Yanira work toward a final product but instead work alongside others within shared parameters to explore creative questions as artists and audience, practitioners, and witnesses, together as one community. "I just couldn't be in a divided space any longer." Yanira emphasized that "making anything for any other reason than to build justice and community no longer made sense to me."

As Yanira slowly challenged her assumptions about "choreographer as author," her identity as an artist shifted. She became engaged in new questions: How to effectively challenge audiences in ways that created the potential for significant impact; how to collaborate in the creation of work that is equitable but also challenges collaborators to take responsibility for our social and personal power? With such deep and important questions destabilizing her habits in both form and content, how would she start to build a new way?

What became clear "was that the most important element to focus on is the relationship between people in a room together." Yanira had always seen the performance space as communal. Ancient cultures performed stories and dances to come together, exchange ideas and news, build empathy, celebrate, and grieve. "At some point, one human being stood in front of another human being and did something that was a reflection of culture, and that [was the start of] a civic space. You're having a conversation about your culture, where you are, where you live, how that's affecting you." Yanira wanted to return to these essential exchanges in her work. She began to explore performance contexts that raised the level of risk for audiences, where they became aware of themselves as members of a community and of the distribution of power within the space of performance and beyond.

Bringing these ideas into action took time, but in 2018, *a canary torsi* hosted their first interdisciplinary performance that was fully based on these principles. Each performance of

Last Audience began with a meal prepared by Yanira of *arroz con gandules*, a dish from her home in Puerto Rico. Audience members were then invited into the theater space to engage with the narrative content of the performance, interacting with design elements—sound, lighting, props—as players who would become equal partners with the performers in the negotiation of the landscape and context of the project.

Interactive theatrical works have ebbed and flowed in popularity over the years and take many forms. Yanira's work is specifically rooted in communal construction that considers the spatial relationships between people and the environment as a way to invite the audience to cocreate the performance of the event as they would in a radical democratic process. She hopes a foundation of practice for all involved will expand beyond the event to the streets, the kitchens, the voting booth, and more.

Many popular "immersive" performances create a world for audiences to explore, similar to a theme park experience. *Last Audience* asks more from its attendees. Here, audiences are invited to commit to full embodiment of themselves, participating in community with others and the space. Active or passive choices made by members of the audience co-define the performance as they do in life outside the context of a show. The show is not a "choose-your-own-adventure" where audiences select from preset options but a container for participatory exploration. It can be uncomfortable when everyone is responsible for being "in charge" of what occurs.

Yanira noted the outcome was variable. "Some people felt transported. Some felt manipulated." She was willing to take that risk. "I was asking them, as Americans, to take responsibility. And while I was not overt about that, as a colonized citizen, I was putting it squarely on my fellow citizens to recognize what they are, in fact, responsible for."

Growing up in a colonized land, Yanira knows firsthand how frightening and difficult such critical conversations are to have inside America. Developing communal skill for accountability takes time and takes trial and error. She explained, "That might mean sometimes that these conversations are not always successful. I can't guarantee success at every single event. I can guarantee that I have tried to be thoughtful."

Ultimately, Yanira said, "[*Last Audience*] did what I wanted it to do. And I was gratified with that. It felt risky. It felt transformative. It felt alive. And I'm in it for that. It pushed. And power was palpable and malleable."

The transition Yanira made from a hierarchical model of creating dance with herself in charge as the choreographer to this more fluid and collaborative way of working put her more in alignment with a near-forgotten inner wisdom. "In many ways, I'm walking back toward my younger self. My younger self knew more. When I came to New York City, I was no expert, and I thought I had to become one. All those years of learning dance techniques took me down paths that maybe weren't 'wrong' but led me away from my purpose."

During the pandemic, *Last Audience* was developed further into additional forms for further engagement. In collaboration with the Museum of Contemporary Art in Chicago, the project was published as a manual for exploration by additional communities, and it was also expanded into a podcast, designed to specifically align with the 2022 US primary and midterm elections, building practice for participation and accountability toward direct civic action.

As Yanira looks to 2024 and beyond, she is interested in the power of much smaller exchanges, the kind, she says, "two people cocreate in a moment" and has meaning "enough to percolate."

With the clarity of purpose her process has uncovered, Yanira has been able to honor a way of working that starts by asking, "What do I have today? What are the things that are around me that seem meaningful? What serves my need to be flexible with my family and time and resources?" Her working method is now an example of the same values she aims to cultivate in communities through her performance projects.

Looking back on her journey thus far, Yanira reflects, "I think I would say to my younger self that she is already the expert. I wish I had been truer to her sooner."

BRAVING CREATIVITY
The pillars of navigate and empower are key to Yanira's time in transition. There will be a time in your life when you realize the discomfort you are experiencing isn't any fault of your own. You didn't do anything wrong, and there isn't anything wrong *with* you. You might notice you don't fit in "here" anymore. You don't belong in this group, in this practice, in this learning community. But before you've accepted it's time to move on, you've turned yourself into a

pretzel to find a way to make it work. Our creativity is stifled when we grasp for purpose in a past that is not moving us toward our future.

NAVIGATE

It's not so easy to change your trajectory on a dime. Even if you've made the brave choice to leave one way of working behind, you'll have to endure more confusion ahead before you arrive at some new place. When Yanira makes the choice to explore a new course, she is not working from a hypothesis.

She has no idea what she will meet in the future. As she follows her heart to discover what matters to her, she endures the discomfort of that blank expanse of space ahead of her. The only compass she can follow is her own desire to find what she knows in her heart is calling her forward. As she "muddles" through a creative process of trial and error, her horizon expands. The work gets risky. She feels alive.

EMPOWER

In the process of creating *a canary torsi*, of becoming a parent, of making the work she cocreates with the communities she cares about, Yanira connects to a much deeper wisdom in her heart that gives her the courage to take a risk and embrace a new way of working. She isn't trying to succeed as a choreographer anymore. She has a new purpose in sight. From this aligned and empowered place, she collaborates with creators and communities who are willing to invite discomfort into the creative process in the service of more intimate, energetic, and transformative connections.

HOW DO YOU BRAVE CREATIVITY?

What happens when you ask the question "What do I have today?" What risks are you willing to take to find more meaning in your work and life? What would your younger self say about the direction your life has taken?

ADA PILAR CRUZ

*I remember an artist saying
that she must draw or paint every day because that way she can
stamp the fact that she exists, and I understood that.*

—ADA PILAR CRUZ, SCULPTOR

Ada felt she had a responsibility to put her stamp on the world from a young age. "My mother had six sisters who were seamstresses, and they absolutely instilled in me that I can't be lazy. I have to do something with my life." The tenets they valued were "we help people. First and foremost, your family, of course; then you have to earn money to pay for your life." Ada said she began to search for work she could tolerate. "I worked at a factory; that was horrible. I worked for lawyers; that was terrible. And so, I wound up making artwork. That was wonderful. Whether or not I had talent was another story." Making art became the way Ada honored her responsibility to make her mark in life.

As a daughter of immigrants from Puerto Rico, Ada Pilar Cruz was born and raised in New York City. A sculptor and arts educator, Ada holds a Master of Fine Arts in sculpture from Cranbrook Academy of Art. She has been a lecturer at the Museum of Modern Art since 1995 in addition to winning residencies at The Studio Museum in Harlem; the Banff Center for the arts in Alberta, Canada; the Arts Exchange in Orissa, India; Nes Residency in Skagastrond, Iceland; and the Tides Institute, Maine; among others. Ada is also a recipient of a Wheeler Foundation Merit Fellowship, a New York Foundation for the Arts Fellowship, and a Brooklyn Children's Museum Fellowship. Moreover, she is a founding member of the Buster Levi Gallery, Cold Spring, NY, and a member of the Taller Boricua print studio in Spanish Harlem, NY.

For the first ten years of her life, Ada had to make the most of the inside of her Bronx apartment. "I was bored out of my mind as a little girl. We didn't have a television, and my mother didn't let us go outside." Ada used her creativity to make things. "I mixed chemicals in the bathroom, made collages, glued stuff together, used mud from outside to build things."

Ada noticed her creative language was different from her friends'. "I wasn't a big doll-player, but I remember being surrounded by girls who played with Barbies. My favorite thing was to create little tchotchkes for the dolls because I didn't have dolls myself. Making the objects was more interesting to me than the dolls were."

Ada was beginning to find out what she would do with her life. "I liked my mark. I liked making my mark." At the same time, she realized at a young age that making things that were different from what people expected or valued wasn't always easy. "My big self-conscious moment was when people thought my creations were ugly. My cousin would laugh and say, 'Well, that knee is backward or that elbow shouldn't face that way. How come this hand is so big?'" Ada recalled making a paper mache puppet in an after-school program. "I thought it was the most incredibly lovely thing. It took me months to make." When she brought it home, she laid it on her bed "like the little girls in the storybooks." She remembered her father coming into the room. "He burst out laughing because, of course, it was monstrous." Even though she can now see why the doll evoked such a response, she said, "I was devastated." Now, she thought, *How do I make it so that other people like it too? How do I get my father to say 'that's beautiful?'*

Ada went to college to study art and find out what she could make that would fulfill the responsibilities she learned from her mother and aunts. When she got there, she was overcome by a feeling of despair over her own self-comparisons to her peers. She didn't feel like her work was good enough. Ada dropped out of school to take law classes, hoping to get a paying job. "That was a disaster." She became increasingly depressed. Not long after, she moved into an apartment in a church building and noticed a flyer for a pottery class being held in the basement of the church. "I signed up for the class. There was no looking back after that. I returned to art and went back to college the next semester."

Even though Ada was finally feeling confident about her work, college wasn't giving her the sense that she could make a living with her art. Then an opportunity caught her attention. A professor was organizing a project with partners in Idyllwild, California. "I asked her how I could get involved," she remembered, "and the professor said, 'Sweetie, just come out and do it.'" Ada purchased a $75 round-trip Greyhound bus ticket and borrowed her cousin's 1950 canvas Boy Scout tent. "It was like a house. I lived in the tent from May until October, mixing glazes and building kilns." It was that experience that helped Ada see that she could make a career out of her work. She kept her job as a paralegal and used the money she earned to go to graduate school. "When I got out with my masters in Fine Art, I knew I'd never have to work in a law firm again. I could teach art and maneuver myself as an artist."

But what she would make was yet unclear. In 1990, Ada stumbled onto something during a year-long residency at The Studio Museum in Harlem. "There was a beautiful African market all along 125th Street, and I would buy beads and fabric headdresses from the vendors." She created a series of figures inspired from the people in the community in which she grew up. "Vendors selling in the street, workers going home from work, waiting for the subway," she said. "Why was I doing that? Why was I making figures of the Black community where I grew up? I don't know that I had the answer then."

What she did have, though, was a sense that her inspiration came from people and the everyday experiences of those people in her life. The lifelong resource of community she grew up in and around was about to vanish. In 1992, Ada and her husband relocated from Washington Heights, New York, to upstate, New York. Ada felt immediately lost. "I'm a city girl. What do you do in a house? I thought it was criminal that there was no public transportation." Also, in her new location, she had no audience for her work and no peers to generate ideas and collaborate with as she had done in the city. "The idea of commuting to the city for community was something I hadn't considered. I couldn't really stay in touch with artists, which was probably the most important thing, because they were my resource. I was in-between keeping a kind of faith and anxious about what would happen next."

Then she got pregnant. "My mother had always said, 'It is the greatest thing, becoming a mother.' Well, she was right." For Ada, having her daughter opened a space she said "was between magic and reality. It was momentous. It was amazing. And I didn't know it until it happened. My mother had told me, but I didn't know."

Now, her everyday experience was her pregnancy. Ada wanted to find a language for this experience so she could mark it in the way she saw it. "I made a series of fetuses." She was interested in the development of the human form. "I was enthralled with this love!" Having a child was a game-changer for Ada, but this new work was controversial. "Oh my God did I get flack. People did not understand. They thought I was antiabortion. So, I just took all the fetus forms and put them in a box."

Raising her infant into her toddler years changed the way Ada worked and the subject of her work. "My daughter became my topic. It was almost subconscious. A year and a half later, I was invited to be in a show of Puerto Rican artists. I made a series called *Divine Babies*. I put iron in them so that they would emanate power."

Even in the cocoon she wrapped herself and her daughter in during the first two years of her child's life, Ada found herself pushing up against norms in the field unintentionally. There came a point when she felt what she represented was no longer valued in the art world. "I was a clay artist—nope;

figurative artist—nope; woman/mother—nope. I checked all of the boxes in the 'no' column." Ada continued to make sculptures. She said, "I had to be persistent. I had to be stubborn about this."

Once ridiculed as a child for making her work, now she felt a familiar sting. "Conceptual art was the intellectual thing people valued then. They thought sentimentality was too easy, you know, too obvious or something." But Ada was determined to make her work. "This is where my language is. Maybe I'm not as sophisticated as you are, but I'm still going to make this; tough shit."

In 1995, Ada began working at MoMA on the weekends as an arts educator, which provided some community and cultural stimulation for her and her family. That job made it possible for her husband to take care of her daughter so Ada could create more sculptures. "I started making more than one or two a year."

Not long after her daughter started school in 1999, Ada's mother died, and in 2000, her father passed away. "Then nine-eleven happened." In response to her grief, she created a series of figures. "I called them *The Lamenters*." Ada made six lamenters for her six aunts, her mother's sisters. Each sister represented part of Ada's childhood growing up. The sculptures, she said, "are crying, holding and doing what lamenters do."

The significance of female lamenters reflects what Ada describes as her mother's sense of responsibility to her family. "She took care of all of us. It was a duty." Ada felt *The Lamenters* were her responsibility to create. "They were all a part of my mother.

That's how I could take care of her. I felt it was my responsibility to make that artwork as a mark of their lives, so I did."

With *The Lamenters*, she received a solo show at the Garrison Art Center art gallery, which introduced her to a new audience of art-buyers. "I met artists. I met people who buy art. I was able to sell figures." During the COVID-19 pandemic, Ada created a series of "Perplexed" figures, which she installed at the storefront window of the Buster Levi Gallery in Cold Spring, NY, looking out toward the street.

Ada is still not sure if she has the answer for why she makes the figures she first started making at the Studio School in 1990. "Every once in a while, I think, *I'm done with the figures*." But then she realizes they help her communicate a language that comes through the work, not ahead of it. "I give them different emotions, mostly subconsciously. It isn't until after they are made that I can relate the figures to my life. It's rare that I plan that. I kind of let it happen. Of whether or not people like them? This is what I want to make, honestly. Which means that I can't concern myself with anything else. Trying to do some other kind of art would be contrived. It wouldn't be real."

BRAVING CREATIVITY

Ada liberates herself from her fear of judgment by navigating with her heart to find an empowered language of her own in the sculptural figures she makes. Over the decades of her career, she has come to feel a belonging in herself and will continue to brave creativity to put her unique stamp on the world.

LIBERATE

From a young age, Ada grappled with the belief her artwork did not belong, that it wasn't good enough. That belief took shape early because of comments her cousins and father made, and it's why she left school and it's what she encountered in the artistic community at points in her career as she made certain kinds of figural works and became a mother.

Ada values what's real and concrete in the emotional malleability of clay. Using any other language as her primary creative medium wouldn't feel authentic to Ada, so she persists despite the pushback she receives at times. Eventually, instead of concerning herself with what other people were making or thinking about her work, she declared her responsibility to honor the "real" in the language of sculpture she speaks.

NAVIGATE

Ada's desire to grow from change—in the case of her early depression and after her move to upstate New York—reveals a kind of persistence she inherited from her family's work ethic and their desire to make a mark with their lives. What drives her is a compelling belief that she has a responsibility to make her mark too. No amount of criticism or rejection will deter her from her purpose.

Ada's choices are led by her heart. When Ada has her daughter, she makes figural art from the pure love she feels for the miracle of life and then the miracle that is her child. When she experiences the weight of extreme personal loss, and much later, the collective grief of the COVID pandemic, Ada creates figures which emerge from the clay with messages that mark those lives.

EMPOWER

Ada embeds love and grief in the figural forms she creates so that they emanate life and a message of having belonged here. The clarity of her values makes it possible for her to create work that holds the tension of the most universal life experiences—love, lamentation, and loss. This is how Ada knows her work is beautiful. What is more real than that?

HOW DO YOU BRAVE CREATIVITY?

What are you stubborn about? What language do you use to make your mark? If you have a responsibility as an artist, what do you think it is?

OPPORTUNITY

You can't get there from where either of us was.
There is no straight route.
Life is so inefficient that way,
and it doesn't really work for me at all.
It works by spirals, squiggles, and ink blots,
looping back over and around like a child's Möbius strip.
—ANNE LAMOTT

When it comes to a process of transition, time is one of those things we can't control; direction is another. While we may not be able to control the speed or direction of our time in transition, we can make choices that contribute to its unfolding. When we allow for the unknowable process of change to be unknowable, and when we accept that it is scary and confusing and painful at times, we can appreciate the wondrous twists and turns we'll take without being concerned with the outcome.

In a conversation I had with *New York Times* arts journalist Jori Finkel about artists whose subject is motherhood, she said of her friend, the photographer Jona Frank, "She was in her fifties by the time she decided to look at her own childhood directly in her work. And she admitted to being somewhat stunned by the obvious realization that 'Oh, yeah, everything that came before it was a rehearsal of sorts, so that I could do this project with this degree of vulnerability and honesty.'"

So often, we attribute our success or failure to our circumstances or to pure luck. And yet, we can exert more influence on the trajectory of our path than sometimes seems possible. If you stay open and curious, experiment with options, and take many small risks, you can create the conditions that will propel you forward, even without having any idea where you are headed. Such propulsions are rarely the result of one single fortuitous event. "It's much more like the wind blowing constantly. Sometimes it's calm, and sometimes it flows in gusts, and sometimes it comes from directions that you didn't even imagine" (Seelig 2018).

As I write this paragraph, a recent client of mine, a fiction writer, texted me to celebrate two recent wins. "I am just so amazed and grateful," she wrote. "I was asked to contribute a short story for an anthology!" She went on to share other good news. "I finally had the sense of self-worth to ask to be paid at my new rate. It felt so easy. Like I was one hundred percent okay with whatever response I got because I knew what I was worth—and the response I got was 'Sounds good. You're worth it.'" My client felt the wind at her back because she stayed open to the unknown and took many small risks that resulted in the outcome about which she was able to exclaim,

"It is just wild what can happen when I put my energy toward what I actually want to do!"

This client is flourishing, and not because of luck. She has found the balance between self-awareness and self-compassion, intuition, playful action, and empowerment. I can tell you that is not where she started. She started completely contracted and fear-bound. Not knowing what the future held, she assumed any choice she made would result in disaster. She felt a strangling responsibility for other people's experiences. She most certainly did not believe she could create opportunities like those that are opening to her now by taking small steps in the spirit of curiosity and play.

When we put a creative process into practice after big change, we create traction that takes us in new directions. Author of *Follow the Meander* Andrew Dietz said, "Linearity is illusory. The more you let go of the expectation of "straightness," the greater your tolerance for ambiguity grows and the stronger your meander muscles become" (Dietz 2020, 9). This is such a critical observation about transition. Artists know this intuitively, but if you've grown up in a culture that prizes straight lines, you might see endings as failures, when, in fact, they invite the kind of experimentation that creates new and exciting opportunities and experiences.

You might feel amazed by your good luck having arrived at some new place in your life that excites you, but look behind you. Notice all the ways you've stayed open and ready to receive the challenges you've faced during your time in transition. The next time you travel an uncertain path, have a little faith in your ability to twist and turn on your way to flourishing.

In the stories that follow, see if you can track the choices the artists made that led them to moments of triumph they could not have planned for. Adele Meyers follows the compass of her heart to island hop onto her most fabulous idea yet; Marta Renzi values failure because it's her path to "cronehood" and dancing outside of society's rules; Abigail and Lily Chapin embark on an ill-advised music tour during the COVID pandemic without an album and find out how much fun you can have taking a risk; Megan Williams exchanges her seniority to begin again and reach for a new and audacious goal.

ADELE MYERS

*What I know for sure is that my feet are on the ground,
and my knees are bent.
That's what I can tell you. Because life is just so shape-shifty,
I'm trying to stay ready.*

—ADELE MYERS, CHOREOGRAPHER

Choreographer Adele Myers's intuition has always been her most powerful guide. "When I was younger, I used to see colors around people. I could know who they are through colors. I know when I get the sense that something has shifted when a portal opens for a message to be received. I don't understand why this works, and I don't know how to open or close it. It's either open or closed. And I can feel it."

Adele Myers is a Miami-based dance maker and the artistic director of Adele Myers and Dancers (AMD), a national touring dance theater company. Adele holds an MFA in Dance from Florida State University and a MA from New York University in Performance Studies. She was an assistant professor of Dance at Tulane University and Connecticut College and teaches part-time at New World School of the Arts in Miami.

In her thirties, Adele landed her first dream job as an assistant professor of dance at Tulane University. "I was done. I was set. Tenure track, thirty years old, renting a place on St. Charles, single, just having the best life ever," she said. And then her best friend introduced her to her now husband, which was "the best background check ever."

At that time, he was a medical resident at Yale New Haven Hospital in Connecticut. When they were ready to move in together, she realized she had assumed that if things progressed, he'd move to New Orleans. When it was clear he would remain in Connecticut, Adele considered the impact leaving New Orleans would have on her career. She questioned her decision to being "done" with her career exploration. She wondered what opportunities she would have as a professional choreographer if she stayed in New Orleans and what she might create if she were closer to New York. "I realized that there were more ways I could grow as an artist in and outside of academia."

Then a portal opened. As Adele and her boyfriend were parting ways at the airport, she said, "I had a very clear, clear feeling. I just said, 'Okay, I'm gonna do it. I'm gonna move.' I had no plans, but I just knew it. That it was right. And I really trust that feeling."

Her colleagues thought she was crazy. "I went into my colleagues' offices and said, 'I'm quitting my job for love!' We weren't engaged or anything. My parents were just like, 'What? You worked so hard to get there.' And I was like, 'Yeah, but love is more important.'"

Soon after Adele relocated to New Haven, she was accepted into the graduate program in Performance Studies at New York University and began bringing dancers together, some of whom were members of her company when she first launched AMD as part of her MFA thesis at Florida State University.

The move from New Orleans was the first in what Adele referred to as "The Three Islands of Big Change." For several years, Adele commuted from New Haven to New York City. "It was hard, but I trusted it."

After a few years, she joined the faculty of Connecticut College as an assistant professor. She spent thirteen years in New Haven building her company and enjoying a seven-year period at Connecticut College, which she refers to as her "dream job." That was when her company started to gain regional and national attention and touring grants. "It just exploded."

Then another change ignited. At forty-three, while her kids were still in elementary school, Adele started going through perimenopause. Everything from the unpredictable hormonal changes to the New England winter weather to the long commutes to New York City and to Connecticut College began taking its toll. "When more than one thing happens simultaneously, I'm just like, 'Wait, what? Where's the ground?'" Those are the moments when she pays close attention to her intuition.

"All of a sudden, I didn't have the energy I had before I had kids. I also started getting depressed." Depression was a feeling entirely foreign to Adele. "I didn't understand depression or why it was happening." She wondered if the winters were influencing her mood. "New England is so gray," she said. One afternoon while she was driving to work, she felt it.

"Something in me said so loudly, 'You're going the wrong way. This isn't right anymore.'"

First, she looked at what might be contributing to how she was feeling both physically and mentally. She was trying to finish a PhD in Performance Studies, be a mom to her two kids, build a touring company, and work her teaching job. "Oh wait, this is mania. This isn't being productive. This is unhealthy and unsustainable."

The second island came into sight when Adele initiated what she called "The Big Quit." By that time, she had completed all but her dissertation for her PhD. "Fuck it, I'm not completing this dissertation." She questioned the rationale for pushing to finish it on top of everything else that was making her feel so overwhelmed. "Like, where is this doctorate going to fit into my life? So I quit that." Then she decided to cut her teaching time in half so she could be more present with her children and her company. And finally, instead of commuting to New York to her company, she brought her company to rehearse in Connecticut. "That worked for a while."

Her depression persisted despite seeking help and the continued shaving back of commitments. She was at the apex of her career as a choreographer when she realized her depression was most likely related to the worsening New England weather. She said, "I need sunshine, literally. Without it, it seems I have no access to joy. And joy? I love it."

Like the reaction of her Tulane colleagues, her Connecticut friends thought leaving New Haven without having a professional plan in place was equally as crazy. She would have to leave her New York dance company behind and start from scratch. Plus, it meant her husband would have to leave his dream job, and their children would have to leave their schools, friends, and everything familiar. But Adele was clear that her quality of life, and the quality of her family's life, had suffered long enough. "Just like love was at the helm when I left New Orleans, this time, it was the quality of life that sunshine would bring."

Adele reminded her family about the deal she made with her husband almost two decades earlier when she decided to leave her job at Tulane so he could stay at Yale New Haven Hospital. "At some point, I will have to leave New Haven. I will do this move for you because this is your dream job. And as much as I love my job at Tulane, I think I got it too early. So I will make this sacrifice, but eventually, you will have to make that same sacrifice. And he forgot about it." She chuckled. "He came around, reluctantly."

They chose Miami for its sunshine and its culture and art, but also because they agreed on the criteria they wanted to meet as a family for their new home. It took some time for her family to adjust, "but eventually, things just fell naturally into place."

Adele had an opportunity to teach as an adjunct at New World School of the Arts, and her husband was offered a position at the University of Miami. Adele spent her first three years creating newly commissioned dance works and gradually building an entirely new company. The five years following that move, Adele's company received commissions, residencies, production, and touring support for a series of new works that won them a coveted National Dance Project Production Grant for the creation and touring of an evening-length dance theater work, T.W.I.S.T (These Women in Space and Time). As soon as that award was granted in 2020, she said, "The pandemic hit. That was the 'third island.' Everything shut down. In that moment, I decided that either this crushes me, or I figure out some other way to look at this than as catastrophic."

This is where Adele's intuition really served her. "None of us in the company knew what the future held. It looked like our whole field was going to collapse." She assembled her company on Zoom and posed a question to them. "What if we make COVID a collaborator? Instead of being mad and frustrated and wasting all this energy and panic, what if we just welcome what COVID asks us to do. If we can't be in a physical space together, can we see it as invitation to think and work differently?"

The company worked in partnership for the next several months on T.W.I.S.T, sharing research via Zoom each week to plant creative seeds together. When the restrictions for assembly were relaxed, they got back in the studio. Any time they hit an obstacle, Adele would say, "We're just going to begin again." For two years during the COVID pandemic, their creative process was informed by what Adele said was a "sense of solidarity and the chemistry between us." The creative process was thrilling for her because she had to invent a way to create work outside of a traditional studio setting and rehearsal practice. "We created a space to be in control of being out of control."

Now, Adele is facing a fourth island whose story is still being written. When T.W.I.S.T premiered in 2021, she expected to have an idea for her next project already incubating in her mind. "But nothing was coming, and it was the first time in my life as a professional choreographer that had happened."

Adele wondered if this block was a result of post-pandemic fatigue. She admits that the previous two years were "just so traumatizing because as much as I wanted to have a positive attitude all the time, it was grizzly, really rough, and I felt depleted. I felt exhausted." She began to wonder "Is it time for a career shift? Because maybe the ideas will just stop coming."

As with COVID, Adele made this unfamiliar blank space her collaborator. The Yard on Martha's Vineyard, a co-commissioner and presenting partner for T.W.I.S.T, invited Adele and her company to spend time in their residency program. "The residency gave us a lot of time to sit and let the portal open up." With that much needed pause, Adele realized suddenly, "What I am starving for as a person right now is radical optimism. I am starving for a better future. I need to feel like there's something really bright and vibrant and grounded and real in the future."

She found a nugget of an idea in a matchbook that she kept from her time in New York three decades earlier. "The front of it said *A World Gone Fabulous*." When she first found that matchbook in a hotel lobby, she called her mother to make a declaration. "At some point, I want to make this work." And here it was again.

Adele imagines starting with a year of research and with community conversations to explore this idea of radical optimism and collective imagining. "And by radical optimism, I'm not talking about what isn't or who can't but what is and who can. Radical optimism is not the same as toxic positivity, and it is actually very hard to create."

Adele has found ground over twenty-five years by listening to her intuition. Each island moved her toward the next one, and she is keenly aware there will be a next one after that. Whenever that change comes, Adele will have her feet on the ground with her knees bent. Now, the ideas are coming. "Thank God a spark happened because now I have that feeling that energy is moving forward."

BRAVING CREATIVITY

Adele navigates by listening to the intuition in her heart and plays with options that prepare for action even without knowing what direction the ground will shift.

NAVIGATE

Navigation is at the heart of Adele's story. Adele maintains an open line of communication between her heart and her head. And although her head has lots of good ideas about strategy, it's her heart she trusts with the big decisions.

Adele senses her intuition kinesthetically. She experiences it as a "forward feeling" in her body that feels "trustworthy." She leads so strongly with her intuition that she refers to her dance company members as "athletes of the heart."

Her awareness of the language of her heart and body is what empowers Adele to change course and leave Tulane and then to leave Connecticut despite external pressure to stay.

Adele notices when the ground underneath her shifts. She becomes aware of the different transitions that are happening simultaneously in her life—perimenopause, depression, children becoming teenagers, COVID pandemic—and which are sending messages she is primed to receive through her intuition.

PLAY

Play is a powerful intention to set when you are facing the unknown. Adele likens the process of playing to maintaining her readiness for a ground shift.

When something seems to shift toward an ending, it's easy to become pessimistic about the future. The fact is our best laid plans will sometimes fail. Play invites failure. Adele doesn't see change as a dead end. She knows intuitively that the next island is just beyond this one. She chooses to surrender the illusion of control over something as uncontrollable as the COVID pandemic in favor of a mindset that can be "in control of being out of control."

In a process of transition, we will miss opportunities because of sabotaging frustration, unhealthy boundaries, exhaustion, self-doubt, depression, anxiety—you name it. There is no shortage of saboteurs on our path. But if we stay ready, we are more likely to receive an opportunity our heart knows is the next big island we'll move to during our time in transition.

EMPOWER

Adele declares her choices at each island juncture. She declares love, she declares quality of life, and she declares radical optimism. By standing in the values that speak to her heart, Adele is able to invite others into a process of collaboration that moves energy. Her willingness to surrender control allows her to stay ready to receive a creative spark.

HOW DO YOU BRAVE CREATIVITY?

What is the portal for your intuition? If you had to name the islands you've hopped in your life, what island are you on now? What's the next one you'll hop to? What is shifting in your life now?

MARTA RENZI

I think failing is a good word related to play…
Because in real play, failure doesn't matter at all.
—MARTA RENZI, DANCE FILMMAKER

Marta Renzi has been documenting the performance of everyday life in dance and film for four decades. Although she has "been doing the same damn thing in the same damn house with the same damn husband," her career has been anything but monotonous. Play and joy have been drivers in Marta's art-making and in her life since she left New York City forty years ago. Marta believes aging holds the promise of an even more creative exuberance. "I've been wishing for cronehood for a while. I'm not supposed to be sexually attractive to you anymore. I don't owe you anything. Youth and sexuality are no longer my stock-in-trade." And what is cronehood exactly then, she wonders? "Is it goofball-ness? A crone lives as she wishes, beyond society's rules, where there are no stakes."

A choreographer and dance film maker, Marta Renzi has made more than fifty dances for her Project Company, creating site-specific work in and for communities across the globe. In 1992, she received a New York Dance & Performance Award—aka "Bessie"—and was the first recipient of a Dancing in the Streets award for her site-specific performances in everyday locations. Marta is a seven-time recipient of the NEA choreographic fellowship and a two-time Bogliasco artist fellow.

Since 2005, she has self-produced over twenty-five short dance films that have won awards in over one hundred festivals both nationally and internationally, including the prestigious Dance on Camera Festival at the Film Society of Lincoln Center. Her feature film, *Her Magnum Opus*, was released in 2017 and presented by Oscar-winning director, the late Jonathan Demme.

Marta's dance work tends toward what she describes as "lighter, joyous, playful, all those kinds of cheerful optimistic things." That might be because she grew up with a lot of space for creative community engagement and play. Her father was one of the founders of the Williamstown Theater Festival in Massachusetts. "We were left to ramble. And we saw more theater than most people did. At the end of the summer, we would collect old shit, and we had a big attic where we'd stick it. So there was material for the arts in the attic."

But she credits her early dance teacher, Joy Ann Dewey [Beinecke], with cementing in her a deep love of play and movement. "My teacher was not a disciplinarian. She was experimental, but not just free-form. She gave us tools like the preclassic dance forms that Martha Graham and Louis Horst developed and then Laban movement analysis, and the experimental stuff from Judson Church." For Marta, the impact of learning both choreography and improvisation, in addition to technique, from the very beginning of her career was consequential. "I don't meet many people whose early teachers taught [all three]. And I think that was huge. I didn't separate them."

The way Dewey taught performance reflected everything that was going on in her personal life related to her children, marriage, or sexuality. "She was an art mother for me. My mother could never have taught me that freedom and that expressivity. My mother was closed-mouthed." When Marta was in New York in the seventies, Dewey followed Marta's work. "She was supportive and critical, you know, like a peer." Marta recalled being sixteen and coming to Dewey's tiny basement studio and opening the door to the experimental scene that was the backdrop to her young training. "I went to the studio for what I thought was our regular Wednesday class in the evening. It's sort of like catching your mother having sex or something. I walked in to find Joy and her age mates leaping around. There were mattresses everywhere. I don't even remember saying anything because, you know, the door opened right into the studio, and I just said 'Oh!'"

In her early thirties, Marta remembers having a dance concert, which was "a really shitty concert." One of her dancers refers to that time in their lives as "the 'dark days.'" That concert was a turning point for Marta. "It wasn't really shitty, but it wasn't really great. It was a lot of work and unsatisfying." She was able to "look around and say, 'Okay, I've been doing this, I'm doing it fine. What's the other parallel line that goes in a life that isn't the next season or the next grant?' I just remember driving home and saying, 'No more company. Now, family will be my company.'"

Marta moved out of Manhattan in 1981 before many other artists were leaving the city for the suburbs. "I moved here, I guess, because of my husband, but also for quiet—separating from what was, at the time, quite exciting, but which I now see as rather toxic as well. You know: the busy city-ambitious-artist bullshit." It was a clear transition for Marta because she didn't identify with being a choreographer who ran a dance company. "Having a dance company is a whole other life from being a choreographer. I mean, a whole job description and identity."

In just the past five years, Marta has had eleven short dance films travel to festivals across the globe, including most recently her 2020 *Fourth of Deny*, a dance film celebrating the life of George Floyd; a pandemic film with the Rhode Island School of Dance, *A Different Day*; and two joyful shorts, *Wait a Minute* (2021) and *Bronx Magic* (2022), both of which have backdrops in New York City streets, its people, and its waterfront.

After so many years and so many films, Marta said, "I've gotten very brazen about not knowing what I'm going to make next." She reflects on the fact that if you are looking for excuses to not do something, you'll always find them. "You just have to show up." This year, she plans to show up in Ireland for the Firkin Crane Dance in Cork and make something. What that will be, she doesn't yet know. Having to pay her own way and her dancers' way isn't a deterrent either. "I don't know what the hell I'm gonna make. It's pretty much all on my own dime. So there's a risk. But I'm not required to make anything at all. So the risk is modified." She sums up her mindset this way now: "I have the ingredients that will make something good. I just try not to burn it."

Marta can keep the spontaneity she thrives on by making short films on a small budget. She was recently the cinematographer for a documentary she is making about friends of hers. "I looked at some of the footage, and I realized when

I really call on myself to be the camera person, I have more skills than I realize. I don't want to raise more money so that I can make larger productions. That is clear to me."

Her spontaneity also comes in messages that remind her to have faith in the process. "I get messages all the time that it's okay, that I can throw myself to the wind and it will work out. I mean, it doesn't always. But it doesn't matter. I'm always rewarded. Maybe that's because I like a mess. Maybe that's because if you put yourself in the hands of something larger, you're letting go of ego. So things become opportunities in a way that they wouldn't if you were pushing too hard. But until something bad happens, I go in with faith in myself and the people I'm working with. Faith that even failure is an opportunity. So far, so good. You know, why muck it up with a bigger crew? I'll muck it up with a bigger crew when there's something that demands that."

Marta recalled a quote from her high school yearbook from the Japanese Zen text Zenrin-kushu. "If you do not get it from yourself, where will you go for it?" Marta's mother was a superintendent of schools, and both she and Dewey taught Marta to trust herself. "I have always known that I'm ultimately my best playmate, my best judge." But what she has learned is that being entirely self-sufficient and muscling through on our own is not always productive. "It's the self in the world. I get it from myself, but not without a lot of support."

Now, she brings the perspective of play with her wherever she goes. At sixty-eight, Marta said, "It's time for pickleball." Having never been an athlete, she wasn't keen on sports. And even though, for her, dancing was athletic, there wasn't the same competition as in sports. "But once I started playing pickleball, when somebody did something goofy on the court, I went, "Oh, it's *play!* They call it *playing* a sport. Having fun trying to do it well but not really giving a shit if it doesn't work well made perfect sense to me. That's where the sport and art intersect."

"There was one day this summer after a pickleball class, I was in the grocery store with my family—my family of origin. I was all warmed up from playing, and I found myself spontaneously dancing—in public, though I hadn't "performed" in years. Who would have thought all the warm up I needed—physical and spiritual—was pickleball? In sneakers. No stakes. I should make this dance: Automatic grocery doors opening in and out…"

BRAVING CREATIVITY

Marta realized early in her career that her path to having a dance company didn't honor her values of joy and play. She navigates in a new direction that puts the pillar of play at the center of her life and work. Now in her mid-sixties, it thrills her to imagine playing outside of society's rules with the liberating perspective that even failure is an opportunity.

NAVIGATION

Marta pushes along a track early in her career toward a destination called "company" and with an identity known as "choreographer," in a business called "dance." It isn't until a ride home after a disappointing concert when she receives a message to make a change that she realizes she is ready to follow her heart's wisdom. When building a dance company no longer feels true to her, she wonders what else is shifting with this change. In this story, we move from learning how Marta trusts her heart's message to make "family her company" to the message to embrace "cronehood." In this transition, her heart wants to express the ultimate freedom, to play in a space beyond society's rules, where nothing feels risky because so little is at stake.

PLAY

How do we know when we should stop pushing? When something isn't working, can we stop "pushing too hard" and give over to the unknown ahead? Play and failure are the same to Marta. Without the fear of failure, the threat of dropping off some cliff, of being wrecked by other people's expectations or judgment, Marta can follow the rules of improvisation. In that kind of play, everything is material—all the mess, all the mistakes, all the seeming dead ends and the magical moments of clarity. Failure, then, isn't an ending; it's an opening. Marta's perspective on failure may be the key to her creative endurance; it's the generous permission she gives herself to "just not burn it."

EMPOWERMENT AND FLOURISHING

Marta approaches her work with the kind of ease and self-confidence that is emblematic of her commitment to stay true to her values for spontaneity, joy, and play. She easily invites collaboration and participation because she has a perspective about mess and mistakes that invites freedom and acceptance. Marta is flourishing in a process that sees age as an opportunity to experience the creative liberation available in "cronehood." With a lifelong self-trust and faith in herself, her collaborators, and the Universe, she can ease into this transition with the kind of curiosity and wonder that makes it possible for her to continue to stretch, stumble, and grow.

HOW DO YOU BRAVE CREATIVITY?

When has failure also been an opportunity? What perspective can you bring to pickleball, grocery shopping, or making a mistake? What tracks of transition are running in parallel in your life today?

ABIGAIL AND LILY CHAPIN

Even if the album is a total failure, we are still facing our fears. The fear put a fire underneath us.

—ABIGAIL CHAPIN

In August 2022, singer songwriters Abigail and Lily Chapin embarked on their first music tour in almost a decade. The closer they got to the tour date, the more onerous the prospect of the tour seemed. They had committed to bringing their families, which included two young children each and their husbands. Abigail said as the tour date approached, "the more my fears came to bear," and prompting thoughts like, "Is this tour stupid? Is it worth it?"

Abigail and Lily Chapin are the descendants of folk music legends and Grammy-Award-winners Harry Chapin (uncle) and Tom Chapin (father). They began singing at an early age with their dad Tom on his children's records and eventually at concerts and benefits around the country. Born in Brooklyn, New York, and raised in the Hudson Valley, the sisters relocated to LA in the early 2000s and started their first band at the encouragement of their half brother, writer and director Jonathan Craven, and with half sister, Jessica Craven. Not long after, the three sisters recorded an acoustic version of Britney Spears' "Toxic," followed later by a series of albums of original material starting with 2008's "Lake Bottom LP," and later became a duo when Jessica left the band after the birth of her child in 2009. They released an album of original songs in 2015, *Today's Not Yesterday*.

Since producing their first full album and an EP that followed in 2018, they returned to New York and became parents. That, along with their day job running a boutique apparel shop in upstate New York, made prioritizing music a challenge. "I can multitask between parenting and the store or parenting and the band, but all three at the same time doesn't feel possible," Abigail said.

During the pandemic, they decided to complete a new album of original songs by spring 2022. From the outset, they knew it would be a difficult commitment to meet. Lily experienced some challenges writing music with a newborn at home. "I have so much guilt taking time and space to create. I am always aware that there is something else that might need my attention." On top of that, "finishing is a really big obstacle for me." To make progress, "I try to remember that when I see my guitar on the wall, I can pause for a second to play for a few moments before my toddler starts banging on it and I have to hang it up again. That little five minutes helps me."

Abigail found she resisted writing new songs. "Nothing is more vulnerable and brings up so much as writing a song," she said. Even when I fully intend to write, I realize that, suddenly, I've deep cleaned my kitchen." The songs on this new album will be another departure from what many fans associate with the Chapin Sisters. Fans' interest in their previous albums of cover songs, like their 2013 tribute album of *A Date With The Everly Brothers*, and for fans who came to their work through their father's and/or uncle's music, has caused the sisters some concern. "Being performers who are daughters and nieces of artists that have public personas made me question my validity as a songwriter for a long time," Lily said.

Abigail agreed. "Our early songs were about my darkest thoughts. That's what you are writing about in your twenties. For me, that is sort of where my aesthetics are still." But in asserting their own style, there is a backlash they have had to face. Abigail recalls fans reacting to those early songs, saying, "Hey, your songs are so sad and depressing, you should be happier!'" That kind of feedback used to pain Abigail and cause her to doubt her intuition. "Now, I feel free to own my songwriting without shame."

In the process of creating the album, they set a new standard for themselves. For Lily, this album represented a choice she has made to focus on creating intimacy with herself and her audience. "What I'm in the process of trying to grapple with is the reason we create at all. What's the point of creating for someone else or for some other audience? My new litmus test for a song is if it's not true, I have to scrap it. If the songwriting goes well, it can be a catharsis, a healing, and that is what I am after."

Though their goal was to finish the album in time for their summer 2022 tour in England, they didn't meet their goal. "We hoped the two would coincide." Despite having not completed the album, feeling concerned about parenting young children on a tour, and fearing the burdensome financial reality of touring and still present COVID travel risks, they decided to continue with the tour anyway.

Given the length of time between their previous tour in 2013 and this one, they entertained the possibility that no one would come to their shows, which were booked in small clubs across the countryside north of London. But people did come. "Every show was full. It surprised us how well the music was received. It surprised us how fun it was to perform and to make new music friends, collaborate with other bands and perform on stage with other people," Lily said.

Abigail said, "It was amazing to see how our music was alive without us even knowing it. Fans were reading about us and listening to our music." The resonance they experienced with these audiences who were so excited to hang out with them in these small venues around England was a welcome confirmation that the risk they took to go on tour was worth it.

They knew that with the family schedule they were keeping on the tour that they wouldn't be able to work out songs and arrangements before their gigs. They set the intention to play a variety of songs they could play with confidence. Lily remembered what her dad, uncles, and grandfather would say before a show. "'Okay, what's your best act?' You have got to make the song choice that will be the best and that the audience will love," she recalled. That was the strategy they used on tour. Together, they ran through their playbook of best songs. "Here's an Everly Brothers song. Here's a Britney Spears song. Here's a new song. Here are some old songs. Here are some folk songs. Here's a British folk song."

By focusing on what they do best, they were able to show up to each gig with self-acceptance and joy. "This is honestly who we are. Yes, our uncle wrote a famous song. Here it is. Yes, we come from a line of folk singers. Here's some folk songs and you're gonna have to sing along. This is honestly who we are," Lily said. Abigail joked, "We have some things about us that are hip and cool. And some things about us that are really not hip and cool. And we presented that in an honest way."

What they have come to learn after almost twenty years of recording and performing is, Abigail said, "When we are having fun, those projects have been our most successful every time." Lily was reminded, too, that she is the only person she has to impress. "I used to look outside a lot more than I do now. Once you kind of let that go, then a lot of the confusion falls away. Other people aren't always going to like what you do, but if you like what you are doing, then you have that satisfaction, and that sense of self-worth."

Abigail was reflecting on the choice to go on tour. "If we had canceled the tour, we would have thought we made the right decision. But, as it happens, we didn't cancel the tour. We went on the tour, and all the things that we were scared about happening, none of them happened."

Before the tour, Abigail said she was proud of them for facing their fears related to writing a new album of honest songs and sacrificing family time to do it. "Even if the album is a total failure, we are still facing our fears." Now that they've been on tour, some of their fears have been allayed. Abigail said, "We didn't know if anybody would come to the shows. And it was a real triumph." If they had listened to their fear, she said, "We would never have known."

BRAVING CREATIVITY

When Lily and Abigail make a choice to stand at the edge of an uncertain creative path, they engage in a personal and creative process to liberate themselves from a stubborn fear of shame. They play by taking risks and empower themselves by rooting their work in their most authentic gift—just being themselves.

LIBERATE

The Chapin Sisters liberate themselves through an intentional process that results in the kind of belonging that reflects all of who they are. What I love about this story is the time they dedicate to their process. As uncomfortable as their resistance to writing their new album feels, they persist in holding space for the work inside of a protected process. They move through their fear of shame because they make space to take the creative risks that feel most authentic.

PLAY

This story shows us how the future rises to meet us in unexpected ways when we step in and try. In hindsight, Abigail and Lily acknowledge how setting a big goal to complete the album in 2022 put in motion a series of smaller steps that resulted in outcomes they couldn't have planned for.

If they didn't commit to the album completion date, they wouldn't have committed to the tour. If they didn't go on the tour, they might not have had the thrill of showing up to full houses. Showing up to full houses with their varied songbook in the way they did was a reminder that they can be true to themselves singing any song.

EMPOWER

What they discover is that completing the album becomes less important than the reward of the empowerment they felt at the conclusion of the tour. The fact that the tour comes before the album is completed seems divined. The tour gives them the proof of their fortitude. The reception they encounter is evidence that what they are creating is so aligned with who they are that it is indisputable. Their validity is no longer subject to shame and doubt.

Committing to the tour gave them the incentive to finish the album of new songs, but now without as much concern for its reception. Showing up on tour with all that was unknown and allowing themselves to accept any outcome was a brave choice, but also a productive one. (Since the interview, the first single, "Bergen Street," off their new album was released in April 2023, the first in five years).

HOW DO YOU BRAVE CREATIVITY?

How does shame keep you from taking risks? What are you afraid will happen if you create what is in your heart? When have you felt validated or seen for a triumph of any size?

MEGAN WILLIAMS

*I've taken for granted the fact
that a lot of things have come my way.
And now time is running out. I'm not a doomsday person.
But at the same time, I only have so many more years where
I would want to be on the stage.*

—MEGAN WILLIAMS, CHOREOGRAPHER

After decades working consistently as an independent dance artist, teacher, and ballet master répétiteur, Megan Williams decided to go to graduate school to become a choreographer. She was fifty-one years old. Megan didn't foresee going back to graduate school until she sat down with dance professor and modern dance luminary Sara Rudner, then chair of the dance department at Sarah Lawrence College. What was scheduled to be a one-hour conversation turned into four hours. "This was someone who I respected enormously, and here she was in front of me having tea. I could never have imagined that this woman I had seen on stage and admired would be so important in the next stage of my development." After that meeting, Megan went home to her husband and said, "I think I need to go to Sarah Lawrence."

Megan Williams began her career in New York as a touring artist in the 1980s. In 1988, she started a ten-year tenure with the Mark Morris Dance Group, after which she became a frequent rehearsal director and guest artist. During that time,

Megan nurtured her teaching career and, after she had her second child, became a faculty member in modern dance at the Conservatory of Dance at Purchase College. Megan has been featured in *Dance Teacher Magazine* and was a 2019 Center for Ballet and the Arts (CBA) Artistic Partnership Initiative Fellow at New York University. She continues her association with MMDG occasionally performing, setting ballets on other companies, and teaching at the Mark Morris Dance Center. Megan is currently on the ballet faculty at Sarah Lawrence College.

Growing up, Megan was drawn to performing, singing, and acting. "I was really into radio. I recorded my own radio shows on a tape recorder. I wrote poetry, and I would perform readings of my poems for my parents. I'd even create shows with my cousins for our parents' entertainment."

Megan knew she had a certain amount of innate talent as a young artist, but she attributed a lot of her success to luck. "I think it's fair to say I had ability" she said, but she wasn't driven toward any specific destination at first. "I had lots of encouragement from people, but there is a little bit of luck in the kind of support I received," she said, referring to the many peers she has met along the way whose families didn't support them. "There was not a lot of money, but there was emotional support."

Megan's parents split up when she was ten. The summer before Megan's sophomore year of high school, her mother moved Megan to her hometown of Canada. A year later, her father died. Megan didn't have any friends in Canada, and her mother knew Megan was angry at her for moving her away from her friends and life in Los Angeles. "She asked me if I'd like to do something before starting public high school to make it up to me and I said, "'I'll dance.'" Megan had built a community of dancer friends in Los Angeles in after-school dance classes. That's what she did in Toronto. "I went to dance class to seek out a home and to find like-minded people."

Megan was never too concerned with the future. "I was a very present-tense kid." She was also ambitious. Megan knew she wanted to be in New York to study dance after high school when someone mentioned that she should go to Juilliard. "*What's that?* I thought. My mother said, 'I think that's a music school.' You know, that was back in the day when there was no internet."

After Juilliard, Megan auditioned a lot, even coming close to landing a role in the original Broadway production of *Cats*. She became a touring freelance artist before joining the Mark Morris Dance Group (MMDG). In 1997, after ten years with MMDG, Megan was ready to start her family. She tried to imagine staying with the group and bringing her kids on tour, but she said, "It just felt so unsatisfying to me." During her time with Mark Morris, she made teaching dance a part of her practice.

When she was pregnant with her second child, she got a job at State University of New York at Purchase in the Dance Conservatory. This was her first institutional teaching position. As she grew into the position over thirteen years, the position didn't grow with her. "By the end of my time there, I was adjunct plus, plus, plus," she said, referring to the level of participation she had in the department, which was significant. "When something would come up, like creating a new course, I would say 'Oh, I'd love to do that. I would love to collaborate with someone in visual arts.' But they were not interested in having me expand my position to include other interests."

At the same time, Megan had teenage boys at home who were "both going through some fairly serious teenage things that were above and beyond maybe some regular things." She realized she could find a more meaningful path forward in the field even while "doing another job at home, which was mothering."

Megan began to wonder about her next move. A friend told her to consult Sara Rudner, who was twenty years her senior, a modern dance luminary, and a founding member and principal dancer with Twyla Tharp's dance company. Megan said one of the things she appreciated about her meeting with Sara was "how present-tense it was. Sara didn't know me, so she was able to just be completely present with who I was right at that moment when I met her, which is unusual in the dance world."

Outside of her peers, the mentors she had worked with up until that point were men. Megan's mother died when she was twenty-seven. "There was something about Sara. She was a strong female person that I didn't have at that moment in my life, and I was longing for that guidance. Then I met her." Megan had no intention of going back to school, but after talking with Sara, she decided to apply.

She had to fill out an application, but she didn't have to audition with the other applicants. That was another present-tense moment. "When I arrived on the first day, none of my classmates had ever seen me before because I didn't audition." Any notion Megan had that she would be extended certain privileges because of her dance pedigree were quickly leveled. "They handed me a schedule and told me that I would be taking contemporary dance three mornings a week at nine o'clock."

As a thirty-plus year veteran dancer and teaching artist before she stepped onto the Sarah Lawrence College campus, Megan said, "I think I came in a little cocky. Maybe it was hubris. I thought I would walk in and get to work on things at the level I thought I was at already. But I was really taken down in a certain way." Megan had to shift gears and adjust to being an equal with students half her age who didn't know anything about her previous dance career.

She remembered having to pick numbers between the eleven MFA students in her cohort to determine who would get first choice of dancers from within the department for their MFA choreographic projects. Megan picked number eleven. "It was an adjustment. I was a student now and equal with everybody here. We're all starting from the same place.'"

By the end of the master's program, Megan felt as if her cohort had become like a family. "We were rolling around on top of each other. I knew what everybody smelled like." There were other things that made the educational experience at Sarah Lawrence exciting. "They don't use mirrors in the dance studios, so I had this freedom that I really had never had before."

Coming out of Juilliard, which had a diverse student body, Megan unconsciously assumed she had already had an education in her own white privilege. She grew up in California and attended a nearly all-white school in Toronto. "Because I was surrounded by this diverse community at Juilliard, I thought, *I got this. I understand all this.*" But some of her classmates at Sarah Lawrence really challenged her. "Sarah Lawrence was already decolonizing the history they were teaching. It was a revelatory period for me. It wasn't just about dancing; it was about looking at the world." Her education at Sarah Lawrence and collaborating with a new community of dance artists was shaping Megan's development as a choreographer.

Megan had to stretch herself in some uncomfortable ways. She recalled her lighting design professor saying to her, "You can do better than this. You are way more creative." Her professors weren't letting Megan ride on her laurels, and that present-tense assessment was the wake-up call she needed to grapple with the aspects of learning that were challenging her. "She expected more from me, and that really struck a deep place." Megan remembered thinking, *I really need to get the most out of this experience. I can't just call it in.*

After graduating with her MFA in 2015, Megan launched Megan Williams Dance Projects (MWDP), which presented its first full-evening premiere of *One Woman Show* at Joe's Pub at the Public Theater in New York City in 2018. The piece, with seven dancers, was an exploration of Hollywood female archetypes and gender norms as they were shaped inside a society led by men. Megan employed various dance forms, music, and costumes to challenge assumptions we still have today about women's roles in society.

When she came off stage at the premiere, a woman said to her, "Boy are you brave!" Megan wasn't certain of what the woman was referring to, but she understood the woman was relating Megan's performance to herself. Megan said, "I guess that's fine." But for her personally, she said, "I haven't really hit that place yet where I feel brave, where I am really pushing out there. I feel like I'm ready for it. And when I do, I won't be relying on all the things that I've spent a career becoming practiced at."

Following *One Woman Show*, Megan self-produced *can I have it without begging* in 2019, a full evening of dance work and a collaboration with composer Eve Beglarian and the Young People's Chorus of NYC, whose premiere was postponed and ultimately canceled in March 2020 due to the pandemic. "I really felt like all my momentum was completely stopped, and I was feeling sorry for myself for a while."

Right now, though, she is grappling with a vision for what's next. "I have some negative voices in my head that make me feel like I don't have something to say in this climate right now. And then I'll have a conversation with a friend or reach out to one person who's also making work or creating something, and I think, *They're following through on this idea they have, why shouldn't I?*"

Megan's antidote to her ambivalence and self-doubt is to just start making things. She created a site-specific dance piece for the Katonah Museum of Art in Westchester County, NY, in 2021 and through a dance residency at the Chase Brock space in Accord, New York, in March 2022.

As she kept moving, an idea that was seeded during the pandemic started to take shape. "I've been toying around with a piece about menopause." In April 2022, Megan performed part of that piece as part of a shared program.

Of a recent commission she completed at the Rye Arts Center in Rye, New York, she says her longtime collaborators tease her. "They tease me about how I start my process. I start everything with the question 'What if we try this?'" In that way, Megan says she stays as present-tense as possible, and she applies the same mantra to her life. "What if I didn't feel regret or resentment? What if I made space for this relationship to be stronger because of what we are going through?"

There is something gentle about that phrase, she says. "It allows me to feel something or for something to reveal itself rather than forcing something to happen."

As she plants these small developmental seeds for an eventual future piece that takes her into brave new territory, a new big change brings her into present-tense again. Her husband became ill. "I want to be completely present for my husband and not have any resentment or regret."

Overall, she says, "I am optimistic, but I am on a dimmer switch. The lights aren't off, but I'm on a low frequency in my creative work and in a high frequency in my care-giving work."

Megan does feel a pull to press further into her discomfort before she won't be on stage anymore. "In the next five years, I'd like to make something substantial." The way she sees her life now is that everything is a seed for something else to grow from. "I have to trust all the knowing I've earned, trust all the experience and all of the things, but also have a little bit more chutzpah to go for what I want in the present moment."

BRAVING CREATIVITY

Megan's story helps us see how the pillars of liberate, navigate, and play are moving her toward a creative risk that feels braver than ever before. When she looks back, she can see how she has created the circumstances for her courage to grow through the choices she has made to take risks and to stay present in the moments that have meaning for her today.

LIBERATE

Graduate school challenges Megan's assumptions that she should be extended certain privileges because of her experience. She thrives in a learning environment that values the "present-tense" experience. The "present-tense" moments she describes offer enormous clarity because they allow her to exist in the moment and surrender attachment to old beliefs and narratives that might limit her possibilities. *What if we try this?* is a perspective that Megan employs in rehearsal. *Try this* is one way Megan makes sure to stay open to new ideas.

NAVIGATE

The moment Megan steps into the interview with Sara Rudner, she feels a shift. That conversation, which came at a time when she was longing for guidance, set Megan on a new course. As she explores creating her own work for the first time in her thirty-year career, she is challenged to find the passion that will give her the courage to take a bigger risk.

She is aware that the transitions "career" and "aging" are running on parallel tracks. Anticipating their convergence is pressing her to stretch into something bigger she knows in her heart she wants to create.

PLAY

As a beginner in graduate school, Megan becomes aware of the potential for her growth and also her reluctance to push past her discomfort. Whatever doubt Megan has in her courage, it is mitigated by the fact that she is willing to try and to begin again. Megan plays with options by collaborating often and taking opportunities to make dances. Those dances plant seeds for what will come. Each step made in the present-tense, is a braver one.

HOW DO YOU BRAVE CREATIVITY?

Would you be willing to be a beginner in your field? When has someone thought you brave? Did you feel brave?

SCARY, THRILLING, MESSY THOUGHTS

When I started writing this book, I wanted to speak with artists who liked to talk about the same things I did. Women who were passionate about making sense of the scary, thrilling, messy changes they faced. I was tentative at first. Artists want to talk about their work, sure. But did they want to discuss the most terrifying, lonely, vulnerable times in their lives with me too? Did they think that *how* they grappled with transitions in their lives was anything special? The answer was, gratefully, yes and yes.

Braving creativity comes down to your ability to stay open during a period of transition after big change. You are rewarded for your endurance with the most valuable resource any empty space can offer: creative freedom. While I called the Five Pillars of Braving Creativity liberate, navigate, play, empower, and flourish, they could be called by other names too. This was the framework I decided upon to locate myself *inside* of a process. Knowing I was inside of a named space, however vast and uncertain, reassured me that I would not feel lost forever.

Understanding this transitional time as a creative *process* made it possible for me to trust in it. By persisting through every messy encounter, after every shame spiral, after every heartbreaking ending, and after every failure, I racked up enough evidence of my courage and my fortitude to believe that I already had enough of everything I truly needed to face my fear of change and separation, even the most final kind.

The artists in this book have shared the various ways they arrived at the courage to take steps forward despite their fear of the unknown path ahead. You'll recognize the tools and strategies they used to stay open during that in-between time as the very same ones they employ when entering an empty space or a blank page or canvas to create their art. With one important difference—big change asks this: *As a result of what you are feeling right now in transition, what risk are you willing to take?* If you are willing to grow, then you are on a path to true flourishing.

Below is a summary of the touchstones used by the artists in the book. It is my hope you will use these touchstones as well as the Five Pillars of Braving Creativity as guideposts to accompany you on your brave creative path forward.

CAPACITY FOR COURAGE

Surrendering and letting go. You are not required to be "superwoman" or "boss lady," or anything other than who you are right now. Antoinette, Cynthia, Maddie, and Adele's stories illustrate this truth: When you are vulnerable and in pain as a result of injury, illness, relationship fracture, or a global pandemic, asking for help and collaboration can help you protect your creative process and make it possible for you to heal, connect, and grow.

Everything is energy. When you take a risk to share the truth of your experience with others, the energy you generate creates movement for everyone. Sara, Yanira, Adele, Marta, Abigail, and Lily talk about the resonance they experience between themselves and their audiences and the Universe when they share work that stimulates dialogue and individual and collective joy, growth, and belonging.

Safe enough. Learn how to create a safe-enough space in which to try something that feels risky. You can't guarantee that every choice you make will feel safe, but as Cynthia, Maddie, Sara, and Yanira do, you can try to create a "safe-enough" space in which to take a risk.

Holding both. Of the many emotions you experience when braving creativity, fear and excitement are the most common. If you feel afraid of taking a risk, check to see if another feeling is also present. The answer might be excitement!

Cynthia, Maddie, Sara, Abigail, and Lily show us how to walk into the creative process or onto the stage holding both.

Why are you here? Expand your perspective to consider your purpose, mission, or vision. Cynthia's purpose is to share her spiritual growth and development process; Yanira's vision is to stimulate collaborative civic dialogue; Sara and Maddie are on a mission to serve women by writing and performing their stories; Marta's mission is to spread the love of play and failure in everyday ways. By empowering yourself to claim your entitlement to your most authentic expression, you serve a larger vision.

Who am I, really? This question asks you to take an honest look at who you are right now, both in your light and your shadows. As you learn to listen and question who you are with care and compassion, you can also sense who you long to become during your time in transition. Antoinette, Cynthia, Eljon, Maddie, Sara, L M, Dipika, and Ada work in the "gap" to find true liberation to move toward courageous expression of who they are becoming after big change.

PERMISSION TO PROCESS

Multiple Transitions. "Parallel tracks" is what Marta refers to when she talks about the many transitions that move, often concurrently, in life as we age and grow. Adele knows when more than one transition is happening at once because it feels as though the ground is shifting under her feet. Cynthia and Megan are tracking similar transitions as they contemplate the impact of empty nesting and aging on their careers. Abigail and Lily navigate young parenthood and launching a new album. Be aware of the transitions you are experiencing so you can sense that you are part of a natural process of endings and beginnings.

Beliefs and Thoughts. Unconscious beliefs are based on assumptions you make about yourself, other people, and the world as a result of your early experiences of real or imagined threat. Thoughts are produced by your brain to fill empty space. Many of your thoughts feed you with repetitive diatribes in step with your beliefs and assumptions. Cynthia, Sara, Eljon, Maddie, Chie, Dipika, Ada, and Abigail and Lily describe the sabotaging impact of their beliefs and thoughts. Question your thoughts first and then see if you can find a limiting belief sabotaging your courage to create something new.

Old Stories. Like beliefs, you carry limiting narratives around about yourself based on messaging or experiences you encounter in childhood. When you find yourself telling a story about yourself that has words like *aren't, doesn't, always, never, won't...* stop yourself. Can you sense a belief or two fueling your narrative? How true is that story today? Is there something that is also true or more so? Every artist in this book had the courage to create a new narrative from the truth of their current experience.

Readiness is not something you wait for; it's something you prepare for by taking many small playful steps. Adele describes readiness as feeling like her "knees are bent" and ready for action. Abigail and Lily do this by setting goals toward completing the album and going on tour, which lead to exciting new outcomes even when the original goal posts move and change. Megan practices staying open and ready by asking "What if" every time she enters a rehearsal space.

Invitations are everywhere. Even brave creatives are sometimes afraid of trying new things. Eljon, Dipika, L M, Yanira, Marta, Megan, and Abigail and Lily demonstrate how to stay curious and open to the invitations and opportunities that arrive at their doorsteps when they are willing and ready to try. The more you try, the more you learn to trust in a future that will rise to meet you with abundant possibilities.

GRAPPLING TOOLS AND STRATEGIES

Compelling commitments. The artists in this book make compelling commitments that demonstrate great fortitude. Dipika speaks of committing to write; Ada's commitment is a responsibility to make her mark; Yanira commits to creating collaborative civic dialogue; Eljon commits to "go full steam ahead." Compelling commitments make it possible to push beyond the goal of creating any single specific work of art to connect to something bigger that has meaning for you.

Values. Putting language to what matters to you is how you begin to stand in your courage. Antoinette values her newfound vulnerability; Julia declares her values of connection and beauty after experiencing the depth of her grief; Chie values artistic intersections; Ada declares her value for making a mark; Megan stands in the value of staying present. What you choose to value now will ensure the choices you make today will have power for you tomorrow.

Playing and failure are two sides of the same coin. When something fails, you are conditioned to view yourself as bad. Antoinette, Sara, Marta, Adele, and Megan show us how play and failure dance together to open up a greater field of possibility than if they'd never made a mistake along the way. Artists who want to grow accept failure as part of a courageous process of personal transformation.

Collaboration. Often, the bravest choice is to work together. Cynthia, Maddie, Sara, and Yanira engage with collaborators that create safe spaces to make bold choices that stretch their capacity to grow bigger than their fear.

Beginning again. Beginning again is at the heart of any transformational process. When something comes to an end, you turn toward a new beginning. Every day and every moment of every day you have a choice to begin again. Yanira starts a new project with the question "What do I have today?" Megan shows us that beginning again is also a mindset that gives us permission to explore as a beginner, even in areas where you might have once felt like an expert.

Listening. Even though you walk around in your body every day and sleep with it at night, you don't always listen to the messages it sends. Learn to pause when intuition speaks through your body. Pay attention! The more you listen, the more you receive. Chie has a resonating experience of Van Gogh's painting that gives her hope; Eljon listens to the Universe's message to declare herself as a playwright; Sara senses from her intuition that something doesn't sound right; L M receives a crucial message about healing that helped her surrender to her grief.

Softening. This is an embodied practice. Just as breathing into a "softening belly" allows you to release unconscious tension in your body, softening to uncertainty releases a kind of mental hanging on to stuck energy. Softening is a warm invitation to meet your discomfort and resistance with compassion and acceptance. When Antoinette, Cynthia, Sara, Chie, Julia, L M, and Dipika soften to resistance, they suffer less and notice options as they naturally arise.

Morsels and muddling are playful ways that Yanira and L M take small steps into the unknown. Some steps taken in small bites, some muddled together, both strategies result in the gentle process of unfolding that shows them a way forward.

Integrate and Instill. Pausing for reflection is necessary for the integration of life experience and to instill the learning that results. Antoinette pauses to consider what new intention she can set to liberate her from gallery voices in her head; Sara used the pandemic time to find out what she must "work through;" Adele finds rest and renewal in a post-pandemic residency that ignites a spark; Abigail and Lily take time to process the learnings on their tour and to celebrate their courage. Taking the time to process our experiences alone and with trusted others is a critical part of any creative process of transition.

You may come to a point in a process of transition after big change when you feel energized to take action that is aligned and on purpose. You will know you are ready to move toward your big vision because you have the skills and support to liberate, navigate, play, and empower yourself. You will have developed the resiliency to dance in the moment with your humanity as it arises because you have cultivated the creative skills to work in a new way that includes all the ways you will practice the Five Pillars of Braving Creativity. You will have a feeling of hopefulness and a trust in the Universe and in yourself that you didn't have before.

TOWARD FLOURISHING

Big change changes our story. Maybe that is why I feel both heartbroken and full of gratitude. During the time I've spent in transition after Eric's death, I discovered how much more capacity I have for growth than I would ever have believed had I rushed the process or trashed it altogether. This time in-between created the space my heart needed to learn to trust that I could move forward with my fear in plain sight. That meant letting go of who I was and how I loved to brave creative new ways of being that honor my life with Eric and the decades of sweetness that we shared together.

Of all the things I've done to stabilize my family and figure things out for myself—in my life before and since Eric died—the most important growth has happened in the moments when I did absolutely "nothing."

I showed up. I listened. I allowed myself to feel. I told the truth. Those were choices I made in transition that felt most risky.

Over the past almost eight years, I have let go of more than I held on to. The more I've allowed my heart to express its longing and its grief, the less separate and the more connected I've felt.

Without a guarantee of how or when you'll arrive at flourishing, you are called to a kind of faith that is rooted in love. You can sense the faith these artists carry with them as they venture toward belonging to themselves in ways that seemed impossible before change. When we feel safe in ourselves, we can create anything.

The years since Eric died were the most difficult years of my life. I still grieve daily. There is an inconsolable place in my heart that opens me up to the most painful and the most honest, loving, sorrowful place in the world. I think that's part of the deal though. If you embrace the tension between love and grief, you will feel the full power of both. That is how you grow bigger.

When you stop resisting change or trying to control the mysterious process of transition that follows, you hear the whisper that believes in your courage to brave creativity on the path to the most meaningful of adventures. Am I still afraid? Yes, of course I am. But I am also excited.

ACKNOWLEDGMENTS

Twenty-five years ago, I received a letter from a choreographer. In it, she wrote "What you've done has magic and alchemy in it." What I did was tell her story in words. I am grateful to the artists within who entrusted their stories to me for this book. If you felt some magic and alchemy in the reading, the credit goes to them. Without their interest and courage, this book would not exist.

I did not walk into or through this ten-month book adventure alone. Thanks to my partner in all criminal thoughts of widowhood, Indira Ranganathan. Knowing you were coming along for this ride gave me the courage to take that first step. To my first and most trusted readers, my sisters and best friends, Sarah F. White and Amylynn Fisher, who helped me have the courage to put the work out there in its early stages and said everything I write is amazing—which is exactly what I needed to hear to keep going. Endless gratitude for the wisdom of my creative bestie, Alison Russo, for bringing in the rear as a champion and thought partner, and for making this a stronger book. Thank you to the storytellers I adore who gave me voice to tell my earliest stories in public—Jill Liflander, Katie Elevitch, and Holly Hughes.

I am grateful to the scholars, educators, and art leaders who spoke with me and helped me find a direction for this book, including Jessica Bockler, Andrew Dietz, Jori Finkel, Eric Maisel, and Sarah Peyton, and my great champion and coach Stacey Brass-Russell.

Truth be told, I would have lost my actual mind if not for Donald Joyce, aka "My Hockey Husband," for taking my son to countless hockey practices and tournaments near and far over the past ten months so I could work on this book.

Thank you to the Creativity Coaching Association and to the Inner MBA Program of Sounds True for reigniting my desire and my vision to do the work I love.

There are women who I have been so blessed to coach over the past three years since I launched my last big change during the COVID pandemic. What we have cocreated in partnership together has its own magic and alchemy and is the reason I have braved the creative path that has led to the completion of this book.

Because we don't do the hard work of change alone, I am indebted to my developmental editor Katie Sigler, and revisions editor Frances Chiu, marketing gurus, and designers at the Creator Institute and Manuscripts LLC for putting your "Never Write Alone" credo to the test and succeeding with flying colors. Many thanks for additional editorial support and counsel from poet/author Lynn Schmeidler and writer/dramaturge Sarah Maxfield.

My heart is always with my in-laws in their grief; holding Eric's memory together for our children has been a great comfort and gift.

Mom, the older I get, the more I marvel at your courage to continue to create through big change. You have taught me to value and celebrate my eccentricities, and I love yours beyond all reason. Your courage to take risks to keep stepping forward and always, always embarking on some new creative project is a great inspiration. Thank you for being my biggest champion.

Partner of the heart, Andy R. Dillon, thank you for making me choose the date to leave my full-time job and then quitting your job in solidarity. But mostly, thank you for being so skillful at helping me feel safe enough to approach a new beginning with an open heart.

Finally, and most dearly, I want to thank my children for being, hands down, my greatest teachers. I sincerely appreciate your feigning partial interest in this project while giving me the space to write because it mattered to you that it mattered to me. May you always feel safe in your heart with all the love you were made with, which is yours to keep and to multiply.

APPENDIX

INTRODUCTION
Kaufman, Scott Barry and Carolyn Gregoire. 2016. *Wired to Create, Unraveling the Mysteries of the Creative Mind.* New York: Tarcher Perigee.

Beck, Martha. 2005. *Follow Your North Star, Chart a Rewarding Path to Realize Your True Life's Calling.* Boulder, Colorado: Sounds True. Audiobook. 14:46:00.

Bridges, William. 2001. *The Way of Transition, Embracing Life's Most Difficult Moments.* Cambridge, MA: Da Capo Press.

Bogart, Anne. 2021. *The Art of Resonance.* London: Bloomsbury Publishing Plc.

CRISIS
Jaouad, Suleika. 2019. "What Almost Dying Taught Me About Living." Filmed April 2019 in Vancouver, BC, Canada. TED video, 17:13 https://www.ted.com/talks/suleika_jaouad_what_almost_dying_taught_me_about_living.

Corman, Maddie. 2019. *Accidentally Brave.* New York: Dramatists Play Service, Inc.

GRIEF
Simon, Tami. 2016. *Being True: What Matters Most in Work, Life & Love.* Boulder, Colorado: Sounds True. Audiobook. 4:17:00.

DESIRE
Brach, Tara. 2021. *Trusting the Gold, Learning to Nurture Your Inner Light.* London: Penguin Random House.

Williams, Reverend Angel Kyodo. 2021. *Facing the Truths that Keep us from Love: A Conversation between Tara and Rev Angel Kyodo Williams*. Talks, Reflections on the Path. 59:57
https://www.tarabrach.com/conversation-facing-the-truths/.

Gilbert, Elizabeth. 2015. *Magic Lessons, Creative Living Beyond Fear.* New York, New York: Riverhead Books.

OPPORTUNITY

Seelig, Tina. 2018. *The Little Risks You Take to Increase Your Luck.* Filmed June 2018 in New York City. TED Salon: Brightline Initiative. 11:21
https://www.ted.com/talks/tina_seelig_the_little_risks_you_can_take_to_increase_your_luck.

Dietz, Andrew. 2020. *Follow the Meander, An Indirect Route to a More Creative Life.* Atlanta, GA: Silent Thunder Press.

www.ingramcontent.com/pod-product-compliance
Lightning Source LLC
LaVergne TN
LVHW012017060526
838201LV00061B/4347